S K I L F

BOWLS

Gwyn John

A & C Black · London

CONTENTS

*With special thanks to
my wife Mayville*

First published 1991 by
A & C Black (Publishers) Limited
35 Bedford Row, London WC1R 4JH

© 1991 Gwyn John

ISBN 0 7136 3447 2

A CIP catalogue record for this book is
available from the British Library.

Acknowledgements
Photographs by Tim Macaire.
Line drawings by Taurus Graphics.

Typeset by Latimer Trend & Company Ltd,
Plymouth.
Printed in Great Britain by
Whitstable Litho Printers Ltd., Whitstable, Kent.

INTRODUCTION

Bowls has no age barriers

The recent growth of the game of bowls has been tremendous. It is now recognised as one of the fastest growing games, with more and more young people of both sexes participating.

One important contributory factor to this growing popularity of the sport is its exposure through television. The vast majority of those who come along simply to try the game do remain with it, so what is the great attraction?

It appeals to all age groups, from teenagers right up to those looking for a sport to help fill retirement years. It is a game that can be played all through the year and its popularity is such that some bowling clubs have a waiting list for membership.

The game of bowls appears easy to play, and the physical demands seem minimal. However, if you consider that a game can last well over two hours and sometimes even longer, then there is

no doubt that the majority of players will leave the green feeling contentedly tired. For each bowl that is played the bowler has to bend down to pick up that bowl before delivery and this represents a good stretching exercise for the back and helps to keep it flexible.

Players must, of necessity, walk from one end of the rink to the other. Even this gentle form of exercise could not be achieved by sitting at home in an armchair.

Some players like to follow their bowl along the green. Their body language will show clearly how totally involved they are in the outcome of the bowl they have delivered. Other problems are forgotten and concentration is total, and this too must be good therapy.

Even before a bowl is delivered, the bowler must decide what kind of shot to play. Having decided, there is the execution of that shot. He may be trying to deliver a bowl which runs in a curved path to an object which can be more than thirty yards away. Added complications may be a strong wind, rain, or a not-too-perfect surface on which to bowl. Indeed, a successful shot requires complete concentration.

The whole body must be perfectly balanced for the delivery action. Complete control over every movement is vital for success, and although the mental application far outweighs the physical effort, both are equally necessary for a good result.

Bowls prides itself on its high level of sportsmanship, and it is quite common to see the opposition applauding the success of an opponent. This recognition and acceptance of there being some people who have more skill than others is an important lesson for life – particularly now that there are so many young people taking up the game.

Not all bowlers want success at club, county or national level. For some the bowling club will become the social centre of their lives.

Bowls has a quiet but forceful discipline about it. There are no written rules to cover etiquette but the young player learns quickly how important a factor this is in the game. Friendliness is the key word – even towards opponents, and the whole ethos of the game can help young players become sportsmen and women in the true sense of the word.

'Will it reach?'

'This has to count!'

The bowler is taking his time to prepare for the shot

'I can see the shot!'

Bowls, then, offers a wide range of positive attributes to an equally wide age range. It is a game where so many can get so much, regardless of ability.

Ambitions within the game will vary enormously. Many bowlers are perfectly happy to turn up at their club on a pleasant afternoon to share in what is commonly referred to as a 'roll-up'. The score is always carefully kept, so even at the very sociable level bowls is still a competitive game.

Other bowlers wish to be recognised as the best bowler in the club, or one of the best in their County, or indeed have ambitions at National or even International level.

Bowls has always demanded great skill, and as the standards of play continue to improve the skill factor becomes increasingly important. If we look at the player who is ambitious and possesses an abundance of natural talent, it would seem that whatever he may wish to achieve should be within his grasp. This is not

always the case since there are several other factors that can have a bearing on the outcome of any game.

For the purposes of this book I will be concentrating on the player who has some five or six years of experience and now wishes to be more competitive and ambitious in outlook, and is preparing for competition. Having made the positive decision to play in touraments and competitions our player must begin to prepare himself.

Note: throughout the book I refer to bowlers individually as 'he'. This should, of course, be taken to mean 'he or she' where appropriate.

Left The bowler can 'feel' he's made a good delivery

Below 'What's happened now?'

PERSONAL PREPARATION

Physical preparation

For a game that seems to demand limited physical input, it may sound a nonsense to speak of physical preparation, but let us look at the facts.

A game can last from two to four hours. Rarely does a bowler sit down during the game; therefore being on one's feet for that period of time can be tiring. This of course does not take into account the constant walking up and down the green. In reality it is only the delivery action that appears not to demand a great physical effort. If tiredness is evident before the end of the game then that can affect performance, and this is not good for any player.

Good care of the feet is essential for prolonged periods of play. Wearing good, comfortable shoes is most important.

Ankle, knee, hip, wrist, elbow and shoulder joints are all important to the bowler. Simple exercises can be carried out to retain suppleness in all of these joints. A brisk half hour walk will do a great deal to help. Gentle bending exercises (with support) to encourage suppleness in knee and hip joints can also be performed quite easily at home.

Standing with the feet slightly apart and raising the arms outwards from the sides to shoulder height and then gently rotating the hands helps shoulder, elbow and wrists to retain a freedom and ease of movement. These exercises are designed to maintain a suppleness of the joints that is so important in the game of bowls.

One possible problem area is the back. Bowls requires a great amount of bending which can be difficult if the back has been allowed to grow stiff. A gentle 'touch the toes' exercise can be introduced into your physical preparation.

During this exercise there should be no jerky or sudden movements, but rather a gentle lowering of the upper body and an even more controlled recovery to an upright position. Even if you cannot quite reach your toes, at least your back has been gently stretched and the muscles kept in trim.

The neck and shoulders can also be aided by dropping the chin on to the chest and then gently moving the head to the right, continuing the circular movement so that the face is looking upward. The head is then brought to the left shoulder and finally the circle is completed with the chin resting again on the chest.

It is feasible for bowlers to devise their own exercises if they feel them to be necessary. Most important is to retain and maintain the free movement of those joints and muscles that are so important in the game.

In the course of some competitions or tournaments, a bowler could be asked to play two or even three games in any one day. This demands greater physical endurance so, as in any major sport, physical preparation should be recognised as an important part of personal preparation.

Mental preparation

There are many bowlers who argue that they never prepare themselves mentally. Perhaps they believe that bowls is a game where this form of preparation is unnecessary. Yet many will agree that their bowling performance is at its best when they 'feel right'. The factors and circumstances that contribute to this feeling will be personal to that particular bowler. The sad fact is that many bowlers do not think deeply enough about those aspects of correct pre-match mental preparation to be able to reproduce them again and again.

Regardless of the opponent, no bowler goes to play with negative thoughts in the forefront of his mind. He does not say to himself 'I am going to lose the game' otherwise he need not bother to play it at all. All players should take a positive approach to any game. They should have confidence in their own ability and be willing and prepared to demonstrate this.

Some bowlers are more prepared than others to discuss their methods of mental preparation, and although some may seem to be of little consequence, it must be remembered that they constitute an important part of that particular player's programme of preparation.

Although bowls can be described as a very sociable sport, there are those who avoid any social contact or chat before a game. They quite readily admit that they prefer to keep themselves to themselves. Their thoughts about the approaching game will be intensely private and personal, but quietness and calm are obviously important factors in their mental preparation. They need not necessarily be described as introvert, but they have found a system or method that provides them with the platform for performing well on the green.

On the other hand, there are those players who prefer a more boisterous approach. The sharing of a joke or mild leg-pulling before a game seems to serve as a boost to their confidence. The last thing they want to be is quiet or withdrawn. To share in a jovial atmosphere suits their particular preparation far better than any other pattern of behaviour. That is not to say that they are any less serious about the game they are about to play, or less intent upon winning.

Other forms of mental preparation include polishing each bowl in turn. The bowls do not need it – but the player does. Again, this is a measured and unruffled form of preparation, accompanied in all probability by regulating the breathing to a slower rate. Some will unpack then repack their bowls bag, checking very carefully every piece of equipment they will need. There is an enforced discipline in this activity which concentrates the mind fully on the task ahead.

These various methods of mental preparation form only a tiny sample of the enormous variety of different approaches adopted by players, but bowlers generally might do well to think more deeply about what occupies their minds before a game. They need to be aware that certain behaviour patterns contribute to good play. Awareness could lead to a recognition of just a few factors that help them with their mental preparation. The next step is, wherever possible, that the bowler be able to reproduce those necessary strategies before an important game.

Even if an ambitious bowler has prepared correctly, both mentally and physically, for a game, care must be taken to ensure that nothing will happen to affect his game plan. One of the most obvious factors will be the surface on which he has to play. The green might be described as 'tricky' or even 'poor', but the player must accept that it is up to him to try to bowl at his best in spite of its condition.

Personality

On a more personal level, an ambitious player may have been drawn to play against a bowler whom he does not particularly like. This could have a detrimental effect upon performance, so the player must try to overcome this obstacle. On the other hand, he may be drawn against an opponent he likes and become too relaxed during the game. This could reflect in his bowling and make it difficult to reach a level of competitiveness necessary to win the game.

Sometimes an outrageous fluke shot can gain a positive advantage for an opponent. Again, discipline of mind must be used to set aside such a lucky outcome and total concentration remain unbroken.

An opponent may rely almost entirely on the use of bowls delivered with increased pace to break up the head and destroy some good drawing bowls. Keep playing good drawing shots on the assumption that the bowls delivered at a faster pace might not always hit the required target. Never allow more aggressive tactics to spoil the strengths of your own game.

Gamesmanship

An opponent could employ some elements of gamesmanship; for example by loud talk as a bowler is about to play his shot, or unnecessary walking up and down the green, or standing alongside the player who has possession of the mat. No player should accept any of these actions, whether deliberate or not. The opponent should be politely informed that not a bowl will be played unless the strictest code of etiquette be observed. This may cause a moment or two of tension between the players, but a bowler is perfectly within his rights to demand an acceptable pattern of behaviour from his opponent, and this must be made clear at the first hint of any such gamesmanship.

Bowlers who progress through a competition may find that towards the final stages there are a growing number of spectators. Some bowlers enjoy an audience. Others find it difficult to come to terms with a number of spectators. Whether extrovert or introvert, the ambitious bowler will undoubtedly come into contact with such conditions and must build into his preparation a tactic that will allow him to withstand such added pressures. Even when the spectators obviously favour the opponent, don't let this affect your performance. Of course, there will be occasions when you meet an opponent in superlative form and you lose the game. Forget that, and prepare yourself for the next important game. Even the great bowlers have suffered defeats but are able to raise themselves from that defeat and programme themselves to meet the next challenge.

The amount of natural ability that each bowler has to offer will vary greatly. However, that is no reason for failing to prepare both mentally and physically for any important game. Bowlers generally agree that when they have felt right they have raised the standard of their game. They must always strive towards this if they wish to compete at a reasonably high level.

Having achieved this state of preparedness they must guard against it being dented in any way. To do this they must be able to detect the signs and symptoms of stress. Unless the bowler recognises stress, then he cannot guard or fight against it.

Some bowlers have a natural ability that allows them to perform very well until they are under stress, when their performance drops off alarmingly. Some who have played at a very high standard admit that there were occasions when they felt under stress. The factors that induced such stress were various and not always to do with the state of the game. What is more important is how each one was able to cope in an individual way.

An ambitious bowler will have to learn to recognise stress when it occurs, as well as being able to develop a personal strategy for dealing with it. One thing that is fairly certain is that the higher the standard of bowling, the greater the chances are that stress will be present. To recognise and be aware of stress allows the bowler to be better able to defend himself, but to pretend that it does not exist is dangerous.

Practice

It is always advisable for any bowler to arrive at a delivery action which is as smooth as possible. Delivery action should be as natural as breathing. It should be part of the 'mechanics' of bowls and should never have to be consciously thought about. Each action is individual, but regardless of differences, the aims and objectives of all deliveries is to get the correct line and length as frequently as possible. This can vary greatly from one playing surface to another, but all bowlers who wish to succeed must learn to read each playing surface and bowl accordingly. With well planned practice, bowlers can improve upon their level of skills and be better prepared to face any conditions.

Let us look at the ambitious bowler purely as a singles player, and follow him through a series of practices, always remembering that bowls is mainly about adjustments. These adjustments in line or length can be minimal, and a minimal adjustment over thirty or more yards is not an easy target to achieve.

'I won't be short'

'I'll just fade it in'

Keep it simple and uncomplicated

It looks so easy!

Singles practice

Weight adjustment

Place a jack at minimum length allowed under the rules of the game. Make sure that the first bowl delivered comes to rest just beyond the jack. The second bowl should rest just beyond the first, with the third and fourth bowls following a similar pattern. (See fig. 1.)

A bowler could achieve very well with no more than four to five feet between the first and the last bowl. This shows very good weight control and the purpose of such practice is that the bowler is consciously thinking of how to increase the pace of the bowl so that it comes to rest at the required distance.

This is achieved by several means. When some bowlers want to reach further up the green they increase the height of their stance on the mat. Others lengthen their backswing. Others lengthen their forward stride to help send the bowl a greater distance. Others say that they increase the speed of the bowling arm from the end of the backswing through to the split second of release. This last reason is possibly the most important ingredient in either increasing the pace of the bowl, or indeed decreasing the pace at which it travels.

The practice is designed to improve minimal adjustment, and the bowler really needs to understand what he actually does to increase or decrease the pace of the bowl. With this he will then have the ability to build into his delivery action such elements as are necessary for controlling the pace of the bowl.

Those who adopt a higher stance on the mat, or indeed those who lengthen their forward stride, are introducing body weight into the delivery action. This is acceptable as long as that body weight is perfectly controlled and does not provide too great an impetus to the bowl. The longer backswing is used by some Australian and New Zealand players, but they still draw to a minimum length jack with the greatest delicacy.

Perhaps the most important factor is that all bowlers should be able to 'feel' the adjustment in pace, no matter how they achieve it, as long as they can reproduce it again and again.

Continue the practice with the jack being placed alongside the fourth or last bowl to be played.

The bowler having returned to the mat begins the exercise anew, but again has to bowl his first bowl just beyond the jack. If the pace of the deliveries is wayward, then the bowler will

Fig. 1

soon run out of green. The player who is able to get the greatest number of bowls on the green before running out of space is controlling the pace of the bowl very well. This practice can now be reversed, with the bowler placing the jack at maximum length, but attempting to bowl the first bowl just short of the jack, the

second slightly shorter, and so on (see fig. 2).

Perhaps one of the worst crimes in the game of bowls is to be short, or not to reach the jack, but there are occasions when a shorter bowl is required. The main function of this exercise is to reinforce that feel for reducing pace in the bowl, and a greater awareness of what is actually taking place, to bring about the required effect.

Some bowlers know instinctively what they need to do in order to increase or decrease the pace of the bowl. However the majority need to apply themselves both mentally and physically to achieve the required result. The exercise described above will help achieve this.

Through purposeful practice the ambitious bowler can be constantly improving the confidence with which he approaches the playing of each shot.

The line

Bowling with correct weight is of no consequence unless the line to the target is also perfect. Consistently good bowling is the result of finding both the correct length and line as often as possible. A bowler will have to read the green quickly in order to get the correct line. There are very few perfect playing surfaces, and a player will have to contend with all manner of variations in line depending upon the green. Sometimes a green can offer one wide swinging hand and one narrow hand. There is no point in stating that a rink is unplayable, because the opponent is faced with exactly the same problems and could demonstrate that he is better equipped to overcome them. An ambitious bowler must exercise a disciplined and determined approach to the differences in playing surfaces so that he bowls to the best of his potential, regardless of the difficulties. Some players may find a hand that suits them well and will exploit this throughout the game, by only playing the less favoured hand when the situation demands it. If the object of the game is to get more scoring bowls into the head than your opponent, keeping to the hand that you favour will probably allow you to bowl with a greater degree of confidence and accuracy.

Fig. 2

'It looks a good line!'

Finding a line

Many find the correct line by choosing a mark such as perhaps a rink marker or any other point of reference on the far bank. Others may choose a spot on the green and make sure that their bowl passes over that spot. There are many different ways adopted by many individual bowlers. Having selected a point, the body must be correctly aligned.

For the right-handed player one basic requirement is to try to line up the right foot with the point of reference chosen. This deliberate placing of the right foot assists the bowler in lining up the whole body with the correct line. To hit the correct line time and time again, lining up the body is essential. Even those bowlers who demonstrate an abundance of natural ability or flair do sometimes fail to find the correct line, and have to re-think and return to basic requirements.

Even when the body has been correctly aligned, care must be taken with the leading foot. If it is placed across the chosen line, then the bowler can tend to hook the delivery arm at the moment of release. This will usually result in the bowl being delivered on a narrow line on the forehand for the right-handed player.

The position of the head is equally important. Looking downwards at the moment of release can result in loss of line. At the opposite end of the scale, a head held too high can result in a poor delivery action, with the bowl being lobbed out of the hand, rather than rolled off the hand. In this case both line and length will probably be lost.

Everything must be correct on the mat before the bowl is released. Sufficient time needs to be given to stance and delivery action so that the player feels the greatest degree of confidence before delivering the bowl.

Line practice

A bowl is delivered to some three-quarter length along the green (a jack is not necessary). The practice is to bowl all of the remaining three bowls so that the second comes into light contact with the first; the third bowl in contact with the second, and the fourth bowl in contact with the third. This exercise is concerned with being able to repeat the same line with each bowl in turn. Repeat this practice using the opposite hand.

The length used can also be varied so that the bowler must read the line required each time and ascertain whether any adjustment of line is required depending on the distance that the first bowl is from the mat.

In the majority of cases bowlers will expect to have some point of reference to which they can bowl, that is, a jack or another bowl. On some occasions it will be necessary to bowl to a position which has no point of reference. The player should practise choosing a particular spot on the green where he wishes his bowl to come to rest, then to practise bowling to that spot.

Draw shot practice

The most basic and important shot in bowls is the draw shot. Variations of this are the yard on shot, the trail shot, the rest shot or the wrest shot. There will also be other shots which require the bowl to be delivered with more pace than the shots described above.

In fig. 3 we can assume that the bowler wishes to remove bowl A from the head; therefore he will have to take a different line than if he were simply drawing to the jack. The right-handed player has elected to play the shot on the forehand with increased weight, to remove bowl A. The player needs to perform this practice successfully a number of times before increasing the degree of difficulty of the exercise.

This can be done by placing another bowl B, as illustrated in fig. 4.

The player must now take great care to ensure that the line he has selected does not result in his bowl making contact with bowl B. If this does happen, he has failed to achieve the objective of removing bowl A.

By adding bowl C the player must now gauge his approach so that an absolutely correct line is vital (fig. 5).

Correct use of such practice not only stores valuable information but can do a great deal to increase the confidence of a player.

The majority of shots, though variations of the draw shot, are played with a pace or speed that has to be perfectly calculated. Others come under the heading of controlled weight or pace.

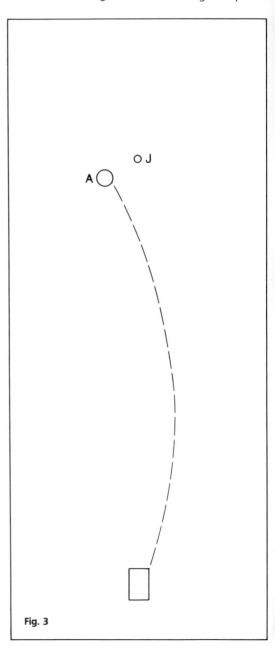

Fig. 3

With each bowl that is played both line and length and weight or pace need to be worked out as accurately as possible. When a shot requires additional pace, then the increased speed of the delivery allows the bowl to travel for a greater distance in a straighter line. This means a different line from the normal draw line has to be found. Pace and accuracy have to be employed in correct proportion to allow the shot to be successful. Such shots should be practised, and the ambitious bowler should be able to play as wide a range of shots as possible.

These are suggestions for just a few practice sessions. Many bowlers devise their own

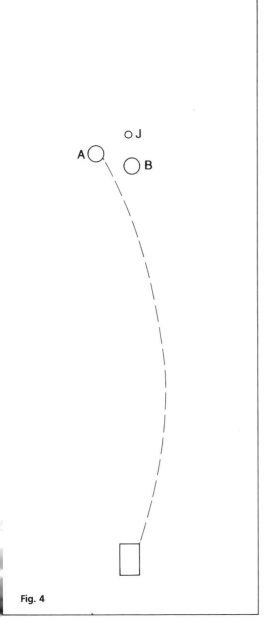

Fig. 4

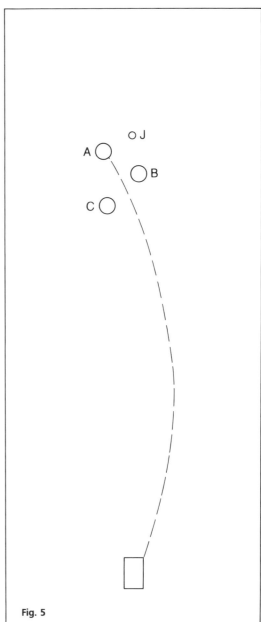

Fig. 5

schedules to concentrate on particular weaknesses. Indeed some even seek the assistance of a qualified bowls coach. Working with a skilled coach can be more beneficial than working or practising alone.

As in all sports, bowls players should prepare themselves thoroughly before the start of any game to eliminate unnecessary errors.

Practice makes perfect

There must be certain aims that the player sets himself with every practice session. Broadly speaking these are to reinforce some skills and to improve upon others.

A player is always aware that the selection of shot can vary widely depending upon the position and juxtaposition of bowls in the head. A player needs to know about impact, angles, contact and the consequent effect of these on individual bowls and their overall effect upon the head in particular. It is advisable, therefore, for any player to first acquaint himself with these probabilities during a practice session rather than be faced with them for the first time during a game situation.

Take as an example an opponent's bowl being a front toucher in actual contact with the jack. Our bowler will want to free the jack by bowling to his opponent's bowl with sufficient pace to allow this to happen. Care must be taken to work out how far the jack might move because, depending upon the positioning of his opponent's bowls in the head, he may still be one or more shots down. It has been shown that when the jack is *not* in actual contact with the bowl it will travel further than if it had been in contact with the bowl. This is an important fact that any bowler needs to remember, and can be learned during a practice session.

The promotion shot

The player in fig. 6 wants to get his bowl A closer to the jack. (Bowl A is on its running surface.) Decisions of line and length must be made.

This shot demands precision, to be well executed and gain a good result. Therefore, it needs to be practised.

The plant shot

The shot in fig. 7 is to play to make contact with bowl B so that it is moved with sufficient impetus to remove bowl A. It is a quite legitimate shot and one frequently attempted.

Not only is the decision one of line and

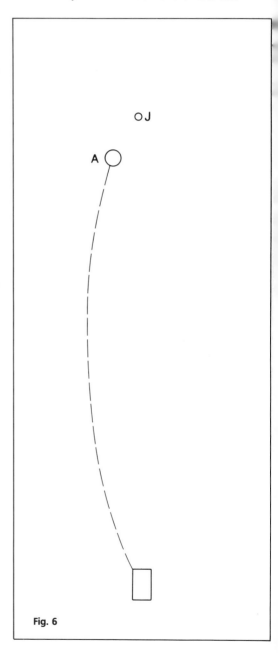

Fig. 6

length, but bowl B must be struck in exactly the correct spot to achieve the perfect result. This shot too needs to be practised.

With both the above examples the bowler will need to deliver the bowl with slightly more pace than if he were drawing to the jack. It has already been suggested that increased weight will need a narrower or tighter line to the target. This serves to illustrate that the game of bowls is one of constant adjustment. Some of these adjustments may be minimal but are the most difficult to achieve.

Any bowler may build in slight variations during a practice session for both exercises mentioned above.

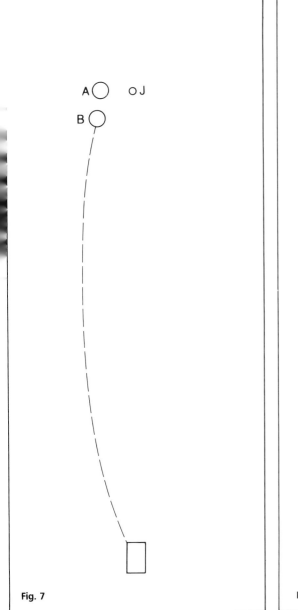

Fig. 7

Fig. 8 Practice for casting the jack

Casting the jack

Accurate and consistent casting of the jack is a skill that can be employed by any player in the game of singles, in an attempt to gain an advantage over the opponent. The following practice can improve skill here. Four jacks, a mat and two pieces of white string about four feet in length are required. Place the mat as for any first end and the two lengths of string as shown in fig. 8 on page 21.

To begin the exercise, the two lengths of string can be set at a yard apart. The object is to bowl all the jacks so that they come to rest in the space between the strings.

The lengths of string can be brought closer together thus making the exercise more demanding. This can be left to the discretion of the player, depending on how much improvement he wishes to gain from the practice. Also, the strings can be positioned anywhere on the rink between minimum and maximum length.

After retrieving the jacks, the bowler can then deliver them towards the mat, attempting to bowl each one to 'mat high'.

In a game of singles nothing is more galling than for a player to bring the mat up the green (as allowed by rule) only to cast the jack into the ditch. This will lose the advantage and may even boost the opponent's confidence.

Playing with increased weight or pace

During a game of singles it is probable that a player will have to deliver a bowl with more pace than that needed simply to reach the jack.

The trail shot

The player wishes to move the jack to point X (see fig. 9). Essentially, he must draw to point X, as opposed to where the jack is situated.

The split shot

The shot illustrated here (see fig. 10) requires more than just drawing weight to achieve a good result.

This is a split shot, where bowls A and B are moved out of the head, with bowl C having

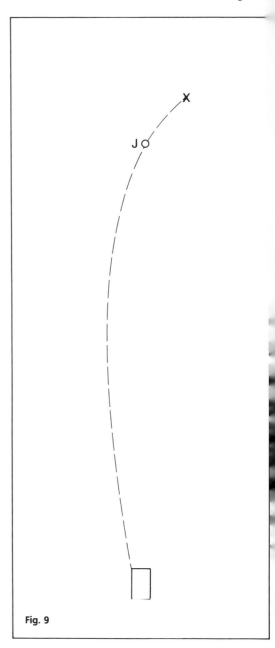

Fig. 9

been delivered with sufficient pace to do this but also to ensure that it comes to rest near the jack.

The weight or pace with which C is delivered is of great importance. The player wants his bowl to end up close to the jack and hopefully to score.

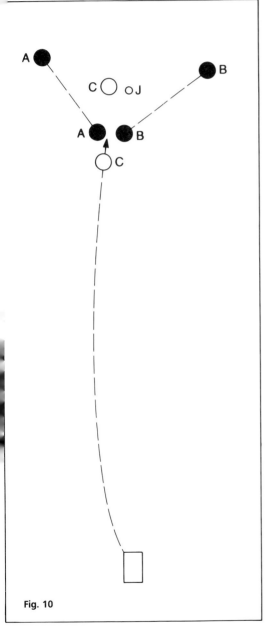

Fig. 10

This shot, well executed, could gain a player a good psychological advantage over any opponent. It would be very worthwhile to practise it.

The draw shot

At any time a bowler may find himself faced with drawing to a minimum length jack, or indeed drawing to come to rest at the very brink of the ditch. However, it must be remembered that a bowler may be faced with a crucial drawing shot when there are already seven bowls in the head. By placing other bowls judiciously, a drawing practice can be made more and more demanding. For example, placing a bowl a yard short of the jack on both the forehand and the backhand could increase the degree of difficulty in drawing to the jack.

There are many permutations of such exercises, but the bowler should bear in mind that to practise difficult shots is more realistic and rewarding than practising those he can play with confidence.

Not all the drawing shots played are directed at the jack. A player may need to draw to a bowl that is two feet beyond the jack. This is still a drawing shot but one requiring a fraction more weight than that applied to arrive at jack high.

There are many variations of the draw shot, but all need to be practised.

The firing shot or drive

Although there are many shots that can be played with a varying amount of pace or controlled weight, the firing shot stands on its own. It is supreme when successful and miserable when missed.

Almost always the bowl has been lost if correct contact has not been achieved. It can be used to drive an opponent's bowl out of the head, sometimes resulting in a good count. It can be used to reduce a high score against, and can also be used to drive the jack out of the confines of the rink, causing a dead end and resulting in a replaying of that end. It is a perfectly legitimate and acceptable shot in the game but one that requires diligent practice.

Everything happens at an increased speed when delivering a drive. All body movement is faster and therefore needs to be strictly controlled. Consideration needs to be made as to what could go wrong. To miss with a drive can have a depressing effect on any player, and provide a morale booster for an opponent.

Each bowler has an optimum weight which he uses to play the drive shot. If he attempts to deliver at a faster pace than his optimum allows, then he will not execute the shot well. A player can only find out about this optimum weight through practice.

Good practice to begin finding this speed is to line up three or four plastic shuttlecocks close to the ditch. The object is to drive each one into the ditch. If they are well spaced out, roughly three to four feet apart, then each shot requires that the player finds a new line. For a right-handed player, the right foot must be placed carefully on the line that the bowler estimates to be the correct one. If the player's calculation of line is slightly off, then a minor adjustment in the positioning of this foot will bring him back on line.

The bowler can attempt this exercise using forehand and backhand, and a progression would be for the shuttlecocks to be replaced by four bowls, each placed some two yards from the ditch. The object now is to push each bowl into the ditch. This exercise may demand a slightly faster delivery. The pace of the bowl leaving the hand will be increased and the bowler will move towards learning more about the optimum weight that he can comfortably employ.

Variations of practices that can be employed are numerous, but the ambitious bowler will at some time have to design a practice where he will bowl into a collection of other bowls placed between him and the jack. He is now 'opening up' the head, and will see that the pace at which his bowl is delivered will be very close to the optimum speed he will find it best to use.

Again he will be gaining that knowledge of feeling the whole delivery action, and most important, the speed at which the delivery arm must travel.

Some bowlers change their delivery stance for a drive or firing shot. Some stand more upright so that, at the moment of release, more body weight is added to the pace of the bowl. This is fine if it works for you.

On occasions a bowler has to play shots of controlled weight. The use of the firing shot is less frequent so it is important that the player learns, through practice, how best to play the drive. It is advisable to limit physical movement to a minimum so that you can concentrate on line and speed of delivery. The combination of correct line and optimum speed are the two most important factors in playing a drive or firing shot, or a shot of controlled weight.

Any approach to practice needs to be disciplined and purposeful, especially if the objective is to improve upon skills. The responsibility rests squarely on you as to how much time you decide to give to practise sessions. Some bowlers claim they are too busy playing the game to have time to practise. However, having already practised a difficult shot will give you extra confidence if you are faced with just such a shot in a proper match.

MATCH PREPARATION

Before the game

Assume that a bowler has prepared thoroughly for an important game and wishes to be successful. Each game must be looked at as being important.

It is vital that the bowler makes sure his preparation is not disturbed in any way. He will be aware of the factors that can upset him, so if possible, these must be avoided. During personal preparation, some players manage to shut themselves off and will allow nothing to affect their ability to play well. This is an enviable state which requires awareness, time and effort to be put into the programme of preparation.

The venue

Always be aware of the precise location of the venue. Don't spoil your pre-match preparation by wasting time finding it and arriving later than planned. Make sure you set ample time aside to arrive comfortably before the start of the game.

As much information as possible needs to be gathered about the playing surface. This can be gained by questioning other bowlers who have had experience of bowling on it, and whose judgement can be respected. Although the outdoor playing surface can change during the course of a game, it is still important to acquire some general information about the green.

Indoor greens can vary according to the different types of carpet that are used, as well as the different underlays. If the speed of the green is fast, it will demand that a wider line be taken.

Flat green bowls (indoor and outdoor) does not allow a practice session immediately before

a game takes place, so it is wise to practise on that particular green some days before you actually play the game.

Arrival

Some players choose to arrive twenty or thirty minutes before the start of the game. How that time is filled is quite important. Some prepare all they will need to play and then quietly observe the green. They prefer to be alone and will not seek conversation. Others are more chatty, appear more relaxed, and by being so exude an air of confidence.

Whatever pattern you adopt on arrival, choose the one best suited to your needs; to your preparation towards playing well. However, don't forget that bowls does expect a degree of courtesy, as well as acceptable etiquette, before, during and after the game.

Experiencing 'butterflies' before a game is quite common and must not be associated with any kind of fear about playing, or its eventual outcome. It indicates that some adrenalin is flowing in readiness to begin bowling. Don't allow anxiety of any kind to take over or this may affect your play.

Trial ends

After the formalities of introduction, and tossing the coin to decide who bowls first, comes the playing of the trial ends. Often bowlers will use a maximum length jack for their trial ends to get some idea of the pace or the speed of the green. You should be learning as much as possible about the playing surface from the four bowls you are allowed to deliver (two bowls in both directions). The importance of the trial ends cannot be emphasised enough. Correct calculations as to line and length should be learned as soon as possible and remembered for the future play. It is possible that at the completion of the trial ends you will prefer one hand to the other and will play as many of your bowls as possible on that hand. No important decision of that sort can be reached unless the playing of the trial ends is treated seriously and with a view to learning as much as possible.

The green and weather conditions

It is obvious to state that weather affects the outdoor playing surface. What is more important is how a bowler reacts to this. Heavy rain can cause the green to become slow so that a tighter or narrower line is necessary, as well as a need for greater pace. Where a green is not totally flat, there could be puddles of water. The extra weight or pace needed to play through such a hazard will need to be carefully calculated. For games that continue in spite of rain, prepare yourself with good quality waterproofs, because if you are at all uncomfortably wet, that will not help your performance. A small towel or chamois leather may be useful in helping to dry off the bowls before delivery. Wet conditions can affect the playing surface quite considerably, but an ambitious bowler will overcome the problems presented by such inclement weather.

Strong sunshine on a close cut and firm playing surface can cause the green to become faster, so that it seems the bowl need only be rolled off the fingers for it to travel a considerable distance. This delicacy of touch presents a problem of control as well as finding a wider line or arc for the bowl to travel. A player who has already practised on such a surface may be able to gain a considerable advantage. Under such playing conditions some bowlers lower their stance to get as close as possible to the playing surface. This can limit the length of the forward step, thereby reducing the

amount of body weight imparted to delivery action. Such fast playing surfaces make great demands upon the skill of any bowler as well as exacting the utmost in concentration.

Strong wind blowing across the rink is probably the most unwelcome aspect of weather. Such a wind may cause the bowl to curve in an exaggerated fashion by sweeping it across the rink, or prevent the inbuilt bias taking effect so that the bowl travels in an almost straight line. Accurate adjustments to line and length will be required to bowl successfully.

Some greens appear to have a 'straight run', where the bowl seems to travel in a straighter line for a longer time before the bias takes effect. Worn patches, especially at either end of the rink, can cause a bowl to pick up speed, because there is less resistance. Shadows from trees or a pavilion may mean a section of the rink being damper and will slow the bowl in its progress. All such quirks of the playing surface will have to be overcome by diligent application and concentration.

'Keep rolling...'

STRESS AND ITS EFFECT ON PERFORMANCE

This chapter has been written by Derek Bell, National Coach for the northern region of the English Bowls Coaching Scheme. He is a former English Indoor Bowling Association Singles Champion, Teesside Masters Singles Champion, bronze medallist at the World Indoor Championship, and English Bowls Players Association Singles Champion.

Stress and anxiety can affect the performance of bowlers just as they can affect other sportsmen and women whatever their field of activity.

To casual observers, the game of bowls comes across as a mildly active pursuit played in a spirit of relaxed and friendly competition. Generally speaking this is the case. When most people take up the game they do so because they see it as a social and healthy form of relaxation which will provide them with enjoyment for years to come.

However, the game can be very competitive, depending on the individual's perception of the importance of winning games. I say the 'individual's perception' because it is from this starting point that any onset of stress appears to arise.

All highly competitive and successful players will at some time feel symptoms of anxiety. Some players are physically sick before a game as well as the more commonplace symptoms of shaking, difficulty with breathing, muscle tension, pounding heart, loss of concentration and lack of self confidence. The symptoms are most prevalent in singles play, but are also experienced in team games by many individuals. Players accept these symptoms as natural, and something to be coped with before and during the normal course of the game.

Before discussing strategies which help to control stress, it is as well to understand just what the phenomenon is. To do this one must first understand to some extent the workings of the nervous system.

The nervous system

The nervous system has four main parts:
1. the brain
2. the spinal cord which is inside the backbone
3. the nerve roots which branch from the backbone
4. the nerves which link the roots to all muscles and organs etc.

The brain passes messages via the spinal cord and nerves to the muscles which are then activated to allow an appropriate movement. This particular facet of the nervous system is called the *voluntary* nervous system. It is under our direct control. We think and act.

The second facet of the nervous system is the *involuntary* nervous system, so called because it is *not* under our direct control. It continues to work without thought. This system controls the heart and all other organ functions.

The involuntary nervous system is itself in two parts:
a. the sympathetic or adrenalin releasing nerves (ENERGY PRODUCER), and
b. the parasympathetic nerves (ENERGY SAVER) which exerts a calming influence on us.

Normally the body functions are kept in balance by the nervous system and we carry on about our business calmly. However, should we feel our safety to be threatened, adrenalin is released into our system and a natural bodily process springs into action. The following physiological reactions take place: heart rate, blood pressure and breathing speeds all increase; muscles tense ready for action; sweat glands are activated to keep the skin supple and also to lose heat; and the bowels and bladder signal the need to go to the toilet in order to lose weight.

Results of anxiety

Unfortunately, if we become worried, particularly about our ability to do well, the body will also respond by producing adrenalin whether required or not and of course the natural physiological responses will occur. If the adrenalin is not dissipated naturally, then manifestations of stress which also include psychological symptoms may well appear.

Manifestations of stress

Physiological
1. Heart rate increase – pounding heart, palpitations
2. Blood pressure increase – hot flushes, dizziness, nausea
3. Breathing speed increase – shallow and irregular
4. Muscle tension – shakiness
   In throat – stammering
   In stomach – churning, butterflies
5. Sweating – hot and clammy
6. Bowels and bladder – need to go to toilet.

Psychological (mental activity increase)
1. Worrying negative thoughts.
2. Inhibitions.
3. Distracted easily.
4. Feelings of lethargy and detachment.

With athletes in competition the effects of even relatively mild stress can lead to poor concentration, poor decision making, lack of confidence and hence poor performance.

How bowlers combat stress

Pre-match preparation

Like other athletes, bowlers are affected by stress at times, even those who have enjoyed many years of success.

All of those who helped with my research preferred to feel normal, relaxed and confident immediately before commencing a game. However, hardly any managed to achieve this ideal frame of mind every time. Generally there was a tendency to be more aroused than this, with a churning stomach and a need to use the toilet more frequently.

In an effort to approach a match in the right frame of mind all had developed pre-match strategies. All, without exception, attempted to put in at least three playing or practice sessions to achieve peak form, in the week leading up to an important game.

When we talked about arrival at the match venue, marked individual differences came to light. Whereas I like to arrive early, sit with a friend, sip a drink and maybe watch a match in progress, a highly talented colleague prefers to arrive late and chat and joke with spectators whilst another prefers to arrive late but only exchange necessary courtesies before getting on with the game.

There are some important points to be learned regarding pre-match preparation.
1. Think about the best games you have played previously.
2. Remember: a. how you felt before these matches and
   b. how you prepared yourself with regard to practice and number of games played leading up to these matches.
3. Use the information you have learned about yourself to prepare a pre-match plan for future games, but always be ready to consider variations to your plan in light of future experience.

I remember playing against David Bryant in the semi-finals of the World Indoor Championships in 1981 at Coatbridge. Up to that game I had won all of my matches and felt on good form. Added to this I had beaten David in our two previous encounters, so I was confident that if I maintained my form I was in with a good chance of winning. About 15 minutes before the next match I was called to the rink for a publicity interview for which I was totally unprepared.

This seemed to unsettle me and I started disastrously by losing a four on the first end and never recovered. As David was in his usual immaculate form, the game was practically a no-contest.

Had I been more prepared for the happenings leading up to the game, I am sure I would have been in the right frame of mind to give a better performance.

Supportive strategies used to overcome stress during games

Games of bowls can take from an hour to about four hours to complete. During the game a player can be involved in actual bowling for less than an eighth of the match time in fours play, to about half the time in a singles match. Particularly in team games there are quite lengthy spells of inactivity, and it is quite commonplace for stress symptoms to appear, especially when a player is not performing well.

I personally feel it useful to watch every bowl bowled, to take an interest in the type of bowls used, notice how heads develop, in short, focus attention on all aspects of the game and especially on the shots you are asked to play.

It is particularly important for the skip to take notice of his players. Usually a player under stress perceives himself as letting the side down. Words of encouragement might help, but talking about the game, focusing attention on aspects of play or describing in detail the shot you want him to play can be more helpful.

If you have prepared well, started confidently and can manage to keep your concentration, you will take the game in your stride and perform well. My research suggests that if things do not go according to plan and stress symptoms do arise, the following support strategies used by successful players may help.

Self-talk

Think positively! Tell yourself you can do it. If you are determined enough you will be confident and succeed.

Deep breathing

A pounding heart and shallow breathing can be overcome by deep breathing. Persuade yourself you are relaxed and you will be.

Slow down

Do not be rushed by your opponent. Take your time on the mat; it is yours until your bowl stops.

Think of the catchword WASP. Wait, absorb and slowly proceed. In singles play walk up and down the green if it helps to slow you down. It also helps you to view the head so that you can focus clearly on your next shot.

An interested spectator!

Quite recently I was skipping a four in a National tie. Even though we were bowling well as a rink, our opponents were better and after losing a good lead we went into the last end six shots down. After more or less conceding the game I found we were lying 4 shots after the first three players had bowled. The opposing skip failed with his first bowl. I drew a fifth shot and followed my bowl to the head so that I could examine the situation after the skip's final bowl. His final shot failed, leaving me an eighteen inch draw to level the game. At this point my heart began to thump, my mouth dried and my breathing became shallow. I walked slowly up the green breathing deeply and telling myself I could draw the shot – after all, I'd done it once. Picking my bowl up and relatively composed, I proceeded to draw the sixth shot. Incidentally, we won the extra end so it always pays to keep trying.

Mental imagery

Look carefully at the head to decide your shot. Imagine your bowl playing the shot (see it in your mind). Now go to the mat and do it.

Muscular relaxation

With practice it is possible to relax muscles which are tense. Hold the muscle in a state of high tension for a few seconds and then relax it. N.B. The National Coaching Foundation have several publications and cassettes on mental imagery and muscular relaxation which are well worth studying.

Blocking distractions and negative thoughts

If distractions and negative thoughts occur then give your brain something concrete to focus on. For instance, examine your bowl, count the number of grips on it, read the serial number and take in the stamp and emblem. Enjoy the feel of the bowl and weigh it in your hand.

I like to look at the jack and estimate its distance. When I go to the head I pace out the distance to check my estimate. All of these activities, together with focusing on the game, help to prevent the brain from creating distractions and thoughts of self doubt.

When I am playing at my best I like to think that my powers of concentration are good and that I am not easily distracted whilst playing. I seem to be able to cocoon myself from everything and get on with the game.

Playing in a Masters Singles final at my home club, I was leading my international opponent by 20 shots to 17 and I had rolled the jack to play the next end. Behind me as I prepared to bowl, I heard a bit of a commotion. Then a

Smoothly away, as rehearsed mentally beforehand

The bowler convinces himself that he can play the shot

spectator began noisily hurling verbal abuse at me and finished by exhorting my opponent to hurry up and get the . . . game over with. I felt positively devastated that this could have happened, but I continued to play though my hands had begun to shake. Curiously enough, I drew my first two bowls close to the jack. My opponent played his first two bowls past the jack, so I tried to match them with my third – I drew to the jack. Again, my opponent, narrowly missing the jack, played through, so with my last bowl I was determined to play a strategic back bowl – I drew to the jack. Almost needless to say, the last bowl carried the jack into the ditch and the game was over.

Not once did I walk up to the head which might have helped me to calm down. Instead I felt almost rooted and so tense that I could not carry out my intentions.

A more extrovert player would probably have turned round and taken the errant spectator to task. What I should have done on reflection was to have stopped play and given myself time to settle down, whilst hopefully an umpire or official had seen to the spectator (who, it turned out, was rather the worse for drink).

Recalling earlier shots played

Often when you are playing you come across situations similar to earlier ends you have played, sometimes on the same green. It helps if you visualise successful shots you have played. You've done it before, so you can do it again.

Buzz words

'Fade' the bowl in, 'drift' round the head are examples of words which can help you or your players to perform the requisite shot successfully. Something like the word 'cannon' or 'explode' can help you to drive straight and true. You can think of words which convey a message to yourself.

Conclusion

All of these strategies are really about confidence, being positive and maintaining concentration. Add to these qualities the state of mind stemming from being fully prepared and you should be assured of a good chance of a good performance.

Bear in mind that you cannot win every game. Bowls is an art and not a science, so things can still go wrong. On the day your opponent may simply play better than you. If he does, admit it to yourself and you may learn something to add to your own game.

Motivation

It could be argued that any bowler who is ambitious to succeed will be well enough motivated – but is it that simple? The professional bowler is still very much in the minority. The vast majority of bowlers are still in full time employment and have to play important games after a day at work. Like all athletes they must bring themselves to a pitch of readiness for that important game they are about to play. What other contributory factors can assist the bowler other than simply the will to win?

Winning against a well known exponent of the game can be regarded as a 'feather in the cap' of the ambitious bowler, and could help to increase the degree of motivation.

While it could be thought that motivation comes entirely from within, it can be surprising the number of extraneous factors that also have some bearing on the process. Even a few words of encouragement can go far towards building up the correct level of motivation. Bowlers will need to feed upon any positive input that might put an edge on their preparation and level of motivation. It could be that one of the spectators is someone the bowler particularly wishes to impress. That is motivation, especially if that person is a County selector. A bowler could have progressed through a competition, playing at venues where there were few, if any interested spectators, but could now be faced with playing in front of quite a large crowd. This could increase the level of motivation for some bowlers. They want to prove themselves, or perhaps indulge in showing off their skills. The venue itself may be one where the bowler has

always played well and because his expectation level of performance will be high, this could easily heighten his motivation.

If any player lacks this motivation, then he has lost the driving force necessary for learning and improving. No bowls coach, however good, can make a player a better bowler unless the player wishes to be so. Motivation produces a need to learn and improve upon basic skills. It should make the bowler aware of the need to practise skills necessary to the game, and especially to practise those areas of his game in which he is less confident.

Motivation is very necessary for any ambitious bowler. It must exist as an integral part of all kinds of preparation. A good player, because of the strength of his motivation, will set himself the task of being as well prepared as he possibly can be for any game. This is achieved through practice either with a coach, or on his own. Bowls is a game that lends itself to personal and individual practice.

The ambitious bowler will need to think positively about practice because he must constantly reinforce his skills, confidence, mastery of the game and the shots in the game. And he must have the correct level of motivation to want to do all of these things.

'Well bowled!'

SKILLS AND TACTICS

Reading an opponent

Opposing players watch each other carefully. Reading an opponent is necessary to build up a profile of his application, determination, reaction to given situations and ability to 'read' the game, and also to find out any area of vulnerability that can be exploited. In the game of singles, a one-to-one confrontation, any weakness in character or skill factor needs to be recognised quickly and used against an opponent at every opportunity. Televised bowls events have provided viewers with close-up shots of players where body language and facial expressions can be clearly read. During a singles game any bowler must constantly be watching for any sign from his opponent which could reveal some uncertainty or lack of conviction or fitful concentration. Such signs can best be revealed by reading how an opponent reacts to:

■ a poor shot he has played
■ a good shot his opponent has played
■ a high count of shots against him
■ a shot he has played quite well, but without the desired result
■ losing an end on a tight measure
■ having some of his good bowls scattered by an opponent's use of a heavier bowl
■ having to correct, following an indifferent delivery
■ missing with a drive or firing shot
■ having to bowl to a head that is not at all in his favour
■ remarks made by spectators
■ frequent visits to the head of bowls by his opponent.

The above represent a fraction of the catalogue of characteristics that any player needs to be aware of in reading an opponent. However, it is well to remember that this is a two-way process. Both players should be learning as much as possible about each other. Any player who shows that it is just not his day is handing the game to the opposition. Showing by facial expressions, or revealing through body language even the gloomiest thoughts, may only serve to boost an opponent's confidence. All athletes seek to gain a psychological advantage whenever possible, and this is equally true in bowls. An advantage of any kind must never be gained through poor etiquette or any form of gamesmanship. Building a bank of information on an opponent, and being able to utilise such information gained, can be an important factor in the consequent outcome of a game.

A psychological profile is necessary, but equally important is the playing profile of any opponent. Even from the playing of the trial ends, an opponent needs to be watched carefully. Consider some of the points below:

■ does he have a preferred length of jack?
■ does he have a preference for the forehand?
■ does he prefer to play on the backhand?
■ does he prefer to draw rather than use weight?
■ when necessary, can he play a bowl with increased pace, and get a good result?
■ can he fire accurately?
■ is he generally just overweight?
■ is he generally just underweight?
■ which is the shot he plays consistently well?

Such information is needed so that the tactical approach of an opponent can be taken into consideration. However, a bowler must never allow an opponent to dictate his approach to the game.

Most players work out some strategy of approach before the start of the game. Such strategy could require a re-think depending upon the playing surface, or even be completely changed depending upon any weakness in the skill factor demonstrated by an opponent. Each player strives to play to his particular strengths, but a prepared strategy can sometimes be superseded by tactical changes brought about by various factors.

Therefore a player should be versatile and adaptable to change during the playing of any game. This presupposes that he has the mental application and skill necessary to achieve these adjustments. Both of these attributes can be strengthened by practice.

Concentration

There are several different definitions of what the word concentration means, but it is important to understand it is a necessary part of any game or sport.

Even more important for an individual is to know how best to apply concentration to his own game. It is not sound practice to associate concentration with negative thoughts, for example the fear of failure. These could be counter-productive, resulting in worry and lack of discipline and clear sighted mental application that is necessary.

How long a bowler is able to concentrate can vary from person to person, so it might be better that it be reserved for the next shot to be played. A certain level of concentration will be present throughout the game, but can be increased to a higher level when you come to the mat and are about to play a shot. This is a critical moment, and it is now that concentration needs to consist of clear thinking.

The following factors can be very damaging to your concentration:

- noise level
- any movement or distraction by other players sharing the green
- partisanship of spectators

The critical moment when concentration needs to be absolute

- an uncomplimentary comment by a spectator
- any sort of minor disagreement during the game
- any disagreement during the day at work or at home
- to have any doubts about your delivery action
- the behaviour of your opponent
- the fact that you may dislike your opponent
- an outrageous fluke by your opponent.

Some of the above could affect your ability to concentrate, but you should try to work out an approach to applying concentration when it is most needed.

The following points may help the process of concentration:

- being prepared both physically and mentally for the game
- having had an agreeable working or domestic day

'What's happened over there?'

- having the self-control to remain calm, in spite of any and all distractions
- having the ability to slow down play – even to regulating and slowing down your breathing
- having a clear picture of the position of bowls in the head
- being completely prepared for the next shot
- being able to conjure up any mental image that supports concentration.

Any intrusive thought will prevent complete concentration. Any tension will transfer itself to the bowling arm and bring about a poor result. Being able to relax mind and body must be a considerable aid to concentration so that the mind is occupied solely with the task in hand and correct information can be passed to the body so the player can function to the best of his ability.

Any learning process requires concentration. The game of bowls is one that demands constant minimal changes or adjustments. Concentration allows a player to quickly recall information that has been stored. This can then be used to help the player when confronted with a difficult shot. No bowler should really attempt to play until that mental and physical readiness is achieved.

Most bowls players will have experienced that sense of feeling absolutely right to play a particular shot. The trick is to reproduce such a feeling time and time again. Any aid that can be employed to ensure this must serve as an important contribution to concentration.

Consistency

Clear minded concentration should function as a great aid to consistency. Consistency of performance can be hard to achieve. It is not simply the degree of consistency through the game, but over a much longer period of time.

The majority of bowlers can play very well on one day and very badly the next. Overall, the more talented and successful bowlers make far fewer errors. The human factor being ever present, mistakes will be made. What is important is how quickly the balance can be redressed, and a greater consistency be achieved.

The game demands that a bowl be delivered on the correct line to arrive at the required length. This may seem simple enough and is just what every bowler attempts to achieve. However, it is easier said than done! Any errors of judgement in reading the green will result in inconsistency and a less than pleasing performance. However, even if the player has made a correct decision as to the line, he still needs to ensure that the bowl will follow that line when it leaves his hand. Every bowler can tell a second after the bowl has left his hand, whether it has been delivered on the correct line, or indeed with the correct weight. They know immediately when something is not quite right. The final movements in the delivery action are very important. Unnecessary movement should not be introduced during the delivery, and the whole action should be kept as simple and straightforward as possible. In many cases more complicated delivery actions are more of a ritual and assist players in feeling ready to bowl.

Delivery actions are individual but the final moments before the bowl leaves the hand are very important in helping the bowler attain correct line and length.

Versatility is another important aspect of consistency. Players need a wide range of shots which they can play with confidence. Even if a particular shot is only used once during a game, its execution needs to be good. To become more versatile and conversant with an ever increasing range of shots means that practice again should play an important part in your timetable.

Consistency is the ability to execute, with a minimum margin of error, a wide variety of shots as and when they are required.

Visualisation

Many bowlers will admit to a better execution of a shot when they can 'see' it in their mind's eye. When such imagery is strong it is a very positive input to the brain, and therefore the messages sent through the nervous system are clear and precise. Some players, on visiting the head, will make a decision as to the shot they are going to play, then look back towards the mat and visualise their bowl on its course along the green and arriving at the desired spot. They may even walk backwards to the mat so that they do not lose sight of the correct line. Important calculations can be reinforced by imagery and the use of such a visual aid can be an important part of any bowler's game.

Confidence

Confidence should be ever present in competitive bowls. It is as important to feel confident when you arrive at a venue as it is when about to play a shot.

This will depend, in some measure, on your pre-match preparation. Confidence is not to be equated with arrogance, or a patronising attitude towards an opponent. All preparation should be aimed at consolidating and promoting

A tight head

personal confidence, and ensuring a first class performance.

Other factors can contribute to the general feeling of confidence. You could have always played well on a particular bowling green. You could have already played and beaten your opponent. You may know of a particular weakness in an opponent's game that can be exploited. Or you could simply be confident of playing very well with consistently good performances.

Confidence is the end product of other contributory factors such as concentration and consistency. Real confidence occurs when these factors combine in the right proportion, to the equation of feeling right. Reaction to feeling so confident will depend upon the individual, but if recognised by any opponent, then that is another positive point in your favour.

During a game of bowls a number of things could happen that destroy a player's confidence.

A fluke shot by an opponent may bring about a good result for that player. There is nothing you can do except to think in very positive terms about your next shot. To reveal even the smallest doubt will only boost your opponent's own confidence. It is difficult to preserve that air of quiet confidence in the face of any outrageous fluke, but you should try to restore any loss of confidence without giving your opponent an advantage.

To sum up, during competition you should demonstrate your powers of concentration, consistency and confidence, and most importantly, your character.

Competitiveness

In bowls, as in all sports, there is a healthy competitiveness between players.

The following are attributes you might expect a competitive bowler to demonstrate:

■ he will never give up
■ he remains unruffled under pressure
■ he does not allow his opponent to dominate
■ he is able to block out any distractions
■ he must be immune to any gamesmanship by his opponent.

As a truly competitive player, you will be prepared mentally and physically before the game. Your approach to your opponent should do nothing to boost their confidence in any way. You should try to be in control of the game, as well as yourself. Demonstrate the ability to make as few errors in selection of shot as possible. You should use aggressive but controlled tactics when the need arises. And, within the laws of the game and the bounds of etiquette, you should use each and every opportunity for gaining any psychological advantage over your opponent. Retain a streak of ruthlessness that is an integral part of competitiveness, without losing your sense of humour or fair play. Your competitiveness will be such that you can analyse, rationalise and repair your game. You will have the ability to learn from, rather than suffer from, defeat. Of course you will be beaten again but if you are committed to pursuing certain goals in bowling at any level of competition then time must be put aside for practice and preparation.

If you have this high level of competitiveness, you will be better motivated to improving all areas of your game.

Will he make it?

Factors affecting a player

Even the most carefully prepared players can have their concentration, consistency and confidence dented by unforeseen factors.

It could be that a bowler has arrived at a venue where there are a number of spectators present. Some may be there to watch an interesting game of bowls, others to offer their support for the home player. Those spectators who are partisan will soon make it clear whom they support and are encouraging to win. As long as this support is kept within the bounds of etiquette, there can be no complaints. However, an over boisterous reaction in favour of one player could weaken the preparation of the opponent. If that player thinks that the supporters are against him then it could affect his play.

Some players could react in a positive way to encouragement for an opponent. It could serve to heighten determination to win against the odds. Whatever your response to this situation, try not to let your confidence be upset.

A person not acquainted with visiting an international bowls series, especially when played indoors, would be astonished by the level of noise generated by the spectators. All players seem to accept this as an integral part of the overall international scene, and cope with it very well indeed.

Spectator support and noise are present at most games. Any ambitious player must prepare some form of strategy for self protection, for ensuring their performance will not be impaired, and that confidence, concentration and consistency will be maintained.

Luck

Most bowlers agree that there are three 'L's in bowls. They are *line, length* and *luck*. There is some measure of luck in almost every game or sport, and its effect can serve to boost any player.

Luck usually results in a far better outcome for a player than was anticipated. That is not to say that the element of luck will be present in every game of bowls. The element most desired would be that of pure skill, but even a shot played with great skill can result in a score against because of fickle fortune.

The very nature of the game lends itself to this. When there are so many bowls clustered together, the slightest touch on one of them can result in a lucky score. Equally, such a slight touch may deflect an almost perfect shot so that no advantage is gained.

As shots are played over a distance of thirty yards or more to pinpoint accuracy, they require excellent judgement of line and length. This is a very demanding skill and the slightest variation could be disastrous, except perhaps when the unforeseen happens, ending in a good result. Even though the player did not actually intend that variation in line or length, the result was good. This degree of luck is quite an acceptable part of the game and has been experienced by almost all players.

Most important is how much the opposing player allows this slice of luck to affect his game. Since nothing can be done to undo the lucky shot he should now concentrate on his next shot and try to gain the advantage once more.

Players will all feel at one time or another that every touch on a bowl or jack seems to go against them. It seems to happen end after end and serves to sap confidence. It is not that they are playing badly, but nothing seems to go right. This is one of the most difficult aspects of bad luck to overcome, but the last thing to do is to give in to it. You should be determined to continue to play as well as possible, without resorting to methods such as bowling at an increased pace or weight in the hope of getting something to go right. Discipline of thought and action will better assist you to overcome the disappointment brought about by bad luck.

Most damaging to any player is to see an opponent get a good result with an outrageous fluke – a shot which is badly executed but very successful. Don't let your opponent's shot damage your own confidence and concentration. Such flukes will occur and what you must do is prepare to play your next bowl, making every effort to concentrate entirely on the task in hand. Whatever strategy you use to overcome such a lucky shot is not important. No player should allow luck to put him off his game.

Things *can* go wrong!

To play such a fluke and think it is your lucky day can be dangerous! You should realise that you cannot expect a repeat performance. Think of it as a one-off event, and nothing more. Players generally must learn how to cope with good luck and not let bad luck affect them adversely.

Gamesmanship

There exists a very fine dividing line between enthusiasm and gamesmanship. The rules of the game as well as the code of etiquette should always be strictly adhered to. The player who follows his bowl to the head may be demonstrating his total involvement, but he may also be contravening the ethics of good etiquette.

Equally, the player who makes repeated visits to examine the state of the head could be applying an added pressure on his opponent, without really meaning to do so. Rarely can such behaviour be described as a deliberate ploy to upset an opponent, but it can certainly turn out that way.

The code of correct behaviour on the green is known to all players; what must be judged carefully is that the fine dividing line between enthusiastic involvement and gamesmanship be scrupulously maintained. If any player believes that he is being subjected to a degree of gamesmanship by his opponent, then he can point out to that player the need for correct behaviour. If this appeal fails, then the umpire can be asked to intervene. This can have a detrimental effect upon the game as a whole – both players could be upset by the incident and consequently the game will not be played at its best or enjoyed by either bowler. However, far worse is not taking action against suspected gamesmanship. The sooner it is tackled the better for all concerned.

The law regarding possession of the rink, for the player about to bowl, is perfectly clear. There must be no undue disturbance, such as noise or movement, that could result in that player executing a less than satisfactory shot. There is nothing to prevent a player from stepping off the mat and even putting down his bowl if he is not satisfied with the conditions. Though many players are a little shy of doing

39

this because they become the centre of attention, they have a perfect right to do it.

If any player attempts a shot when conditions are less than satisfactory, and plays a poor shot, then his confidence can be seriously dented.

Bowls often presents itself as a leisurely pursuit, but there is also an intense competitiveness about the game. It is also a 'thinking' game and a player should never accept any action or behaviour from an opponent that could damage his own clear thinking process. Whether an element of gamesmanship is applied inadvertently or deliberately, neither is acceptable. Immediate action should be taken. No player should be allowed to gain any kind of advantage by disregarding the laws of the game or the principles of etiquette. A player must also be firm in applying self discipline to his own game, and be determined to play without bending or stretching any rule.

Fortunately, the element of gamesmanship is not very evident in bowls. However, any player must be able to recognise it and be prepared to act, so the integrity of the game is preserved and his own game protected.

Goal setting

Players need to remember that bowls is becoming a more and more competitive sport. These days some bowlers have a professional status. Even if an ambitious bowler is not striving that high, he must still adopt a professional attitude to preparation, and part of this must be practice put in on the green. Success can feed ambition, but this will be difficult if correct preparation is lacking. Preparation such as physical fitness and purposeful practice are closely allied to mental preparation because they demand the discipline of mind and body.

Spending time away from the game situation, but working hard at practice under the guidance of a coach can be a very important part of preparation. Coach and player can then discuss areas of practice that will help the player improve. Such practice could be one of bowling

with controlled weight. A coach will first discuss with the bowler what he considers would be sufficient weight or pace to achieve the required result. A coach may prepare the following situations:

- the split shot
- the take out shot
- the promotion shot
- the plant shot.

Obviously not all would be on the centre line, so the player would have to find the correct line for a successful outcome.

The above represents only one area of the game, but if the player has admitted that he is not too happy when having to play with controlled weight, then working at such an exercise must be regarded as strengthening his game as a whole.

Although some bowlers might prefer to practise alone, experience in goal setting has shown that more can be gained when a player works with a coach.

A coach can be analytical without being critical. He needs to be remedial with ideas and suggestions. He can certainly act as a catalyst for an improved degree of motivation and must become totally involved in the goal setting exercise.

A coach and player should meet at regular intervals to discuss each game that the player has undertaken. By doing so, the player gets the maximum benefit and both coach and player can formulate purposeful practices for the forthcoming sessions.

No two heads in bowls will ever be the same, therefore a player can meet with a variety of tests to his skill. Players need to mentally store important information about the execution of shots as well as the outcome. Storing of important information is a very necessary part of any player's completeness as a competitor. Such information can be shared with the coach so that he in turn can extend the scope of future practices.

As a result of a well planned and programmed goal setting exercise, a player will find himself the richer in experience as well as being better prepared to deal with situations as they arise during a competition.

MATCH PLAY

The first end

The mat must be placed according to rule for the first end. The player to deliver the jack will have already decided on the length, or distance from the mat to the jack, that may be best suited to him. Now he has to deliver the jack as close as possible to the length he has chosen. This is an important part of the game and the skill of bowling the jack is one never to be underrated.

Each time a player comes to the mat he must decide whether to bowl forehand or backhand and the pace or weight of the bowl. All bowlers know immediately the bowl has left their hand whether it is good or not.

Even at this early stage a player will have learned something about the playing surface which will help him select the correct line. Having done this he then needs to ensure that the right foot (for a right handed player) is pointing along that line, and that his whole body is aligned. The decision of weight or pace is determined by the speed of the arm coming through from the end of the backswing to the split second of release. The bowl is delivered

Placing the mat

'That's a good weight!'

and the player knows almost instinctively if he stands a good chance of success.

The best reply to a good first bowl by an opponent is to bowl an even better shot. This is best achieved if you feel quietly confident of success.

A ploy that many bowlers use is to have a clear mental picture of the shot they are about to play. This form of visualisation is a very important asset. The expression, 'I can see it that way' is reasonably common in the game.

If the opponent's bowl comes to rest, on a perfect line, some six inches short of the jack, some players find this a difficult shot to follow, since they cannot see the jack. The bowl that comes to rest so that it blots out a view of the jack is not the only one disliked by bowlers. Many do not like to see an opponent's bowl come to rest just behind the jack. All bowlers have certain dislikes as to the positioning of an opponent's bowl, and must be diligent in practising those areas that are less than satisfactory.

A good first bowl helps to lift the morale of any player, and in turn puts pressure on an opponent. However, pressure must not give way to panic.

The next player should attempt to beat his opponent's first bowl, or to bowl a very good second. The worst thing in this situation would

be to bowl short, that is, a bowl that does not reach the head. In fierce competition there is no place for wasted bowls or shots poorly executed.

The bowling needs to be tight and controlled, depending as much on mental attitude as physical performance. Decisions need to be made with clarity of attitude and approach, never allowing an opponent's performance to dominate the clear thinking necessary for selecting the next shot to be played.

Selection of shot

In fig. 11, player A has delivered all four bowls and holds two shots. Player B has one bowl to play and must select one shot from a variety of options.

1. To draw the shot on the backhand, between bowls W and A.
2. To touch bowl W on the inside and come to rest near the jack.
3. To make a fuller contact on bowl W and promote it to shot.
4. To play on to bowl B on the forehand with sufficient pace to dislodge it, with his own taking its place for shot.

5. To play for the gap between A and B on the forehand with sufficient weight to push both away from their scoring positions.

Even if the list of options is closed at 5 (the first end), there are several other options to getting the shot, and players will generally

Fig. 11

choose one according to their own strengths.

If player B is a good drawing player, he may choose option 1. If he plays controlled weight consistently well, he could select option 5. Another consideration that must be included in the equation of decision making is the playing surface. Is it fast or slow? Is there one narrow hand, whilst the other takes a wider line of approach? Bowls demands quite outstanding skills and generally the player with the greatest command of the required skills will be better able to make a positive shot selection, and better equipped to execute it well.

Assuming player B wins the first end with his last bowl, then he has the right to place the mat for the second end. If he changes its position, then he is employing certain tactics in order to gain an advantage over his opponent, since this could mean changing the length of the jack. The mat may not always be moved for this reason alone. A bowler may have noticed a particular spot on the rink which causes the bowl to behave in a slightly less than true fashion. Moving the mat could be his way of trying to avoid such a nuisance spot.

The second end

The second end begins with B playing to this preferred length. He may hope that this preference is not shared by his opponent, and will watch carefully when the latter comes to bowl.

The object of each end is to attempt to get as many scoring bowls into the head as skill will allow. Scoring bowls need not be clustered at the head or around the jack. Such accurate and precise play could be destroyed by one firing shot or drive, since a cluster of bowls can present a considerable target for any opponent. It could be better to think of scoring bowls being not always too close to the jack. This approach seeks to place bowls to score as many shots as possible and, at the same time, prevent a high score against.

In the following situation (see fig. 12) six bowls have already been delivered, three by each player, and it might be better to think in terms of cover.

Player A can draw another shot, possibly

increasing the pressure upon player B. However, the three opposing bowls are in such a position that a movement of the jack towards them could mean player A having a number of shots scored against him. Therefore player A's last bowl could come to rest against the bowls of player B, or at least between them and the jack.

If player A does this successfully, he has provided himself with important cover. However, player B still has more than one option for his last bowl. If he plays with controlled weight to move the jack four to six feet back he could bring into the count some of the bowls he has already played.

player B

player A

Fig. 12

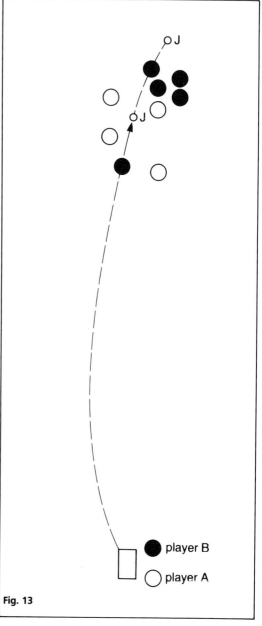

player B

player A

Fig. 13

'Last bowls' shot!'

In fig. 13 player A could have tried to block his opponent's access to the jack by placing his last bowl in front of the jack. A blocking bowl can be difficult to play because the distance it travels along the rink is critical. It need not be too close to the jack since this would only increase the target area for an opponent. To be effective it must prevent access to the jack and deny an opponent the option of moving the jack by using controlled weight.

The timing of shot selection

One of the most important factors in decision making is timing. In general terms, it would not be good practice to leave the crucial decision of shot selection until there is just one bowl left to play. In a game of singles many players might find themselves in such a position, following some good bowling by an opponent. This is a very different situation, and demands that any player must demonstrate courage and determination to redress the situation at the head after careful calculation of all the options available.

Whenever possible, the decision to play a particular shot should be taken sooner rather than later. For example, a player has played his

first two bowls very close to the jack, whilst his opponent has played only one bowl and has not achieved a great deal. The opponent could now decide to play with controlled weight, or an out and out drive, depending upon the score. Whichever, he has now decided to wrest the advantage away from his opponent. Some will argue that the 'name of the game' is drawing, but the firing shot is a perfectly legitimate and acceptable option. When played well at such an early stage of an end, it can do a great deal to dent the confidence of any opponent, as well as having a very positive effect, for the better, on the player who was successful.

Pressure of play

If the winning of an end of bowls is the most important result to achieve, perhaps the next most important is to ensure that the score against is kept as low as possible. A second bowl may lack the glamour of a shot bowl, but it is still an important shot to play. It could mean playing a shot to rest an opponent's bowl or bowls. It could mean playing to an area of the rink, following considerable movement of the jack, where the player had not needed to bowl previously. Or it could mean having to play to the very edge of the ditch to prevent a high count of shots against. To be successful, line and length must be judged exactly. Added to this is the pressure of realising what can happen if the shot fails. Any ambitious bowler must learn how to recognise and cope with pressure of any kind.

The reaction to a pressure situation will vary with each individual, but a bowler who sets out to achieve a reputation as a singles player will, undoubtedly, meet such pressure. The important point is to prepare some kind of strategy to deal with it.

Even during a game the degree of pressure can vary. Any form of physical tension can contribute to a poor result. The mechanics of the delivery action must not be allowed to be adversely affected by any tension in neck, shoulders or bowling arm. The delivery needs to be as free flowing and as smooth as possible, and the bowl should be delivered only when the player knows he is both mentally and physically prepared. Of course, this applies to every bowl played during a game, but without doubt there will be those special or pressure occasions when everything will have to be exactly right.

Playing in front of spectators has already been mentioned, and can be an added dimension of pressure. If a bowler is worried about spectators being present at a game, it may help to speak with another bowler who has more experience of playing under such conditions. In seeking some kind of information the ambitious bowler is taking a serious step in preparation for competition.

Tactical play

Applying pressure on an opponent (without bending the rules or breaking the bounds of etiquette) is an acceptable tactic. Some opponents may be demoralised if you play with great consistency.

Other players are very boisterous and on occasions can be noisy. They may not seek to gain any advantage, but are simply demonstrating their own approach to the game. The less extrovert player must never allow this to pressurise his game.

By comparison the strong, silent type will give the appearance of quiet calm, will not be aloof, but will certainly set himself apart.

The above represent a small selection of the different approaches and attitudes of players. Such behaviour patterns can be an important part of general tactics. In broad terms, the tactics applied to actual bowling during any game can be divided into two categories.

First are the tactics that a player has chosen to adopt, and, secondly, are those tactics forced upon him by an opponent.

Early in the game, once the reading of the green has been completed, a player must decide:

- the length best suited to him and
- the hand he decides is the most true.

A player will play his bowls on his favoured hand whenever possible, even if his opponent chooses the same hand.

All players must be alert and aware of any subtle tactical changes that can take place during any game. Such tactical changes present a challenge which must be met with quiet confidence.

In fig. 14 the length of jack is close to the maximum allowed by rule. Fig. 15 shows the mat moved well up the rink, and the distance between mat and jack is considerably less.

A player should consider what the different lengths of jack mean in terms of the behaviour of his bowl. If we assume that both players are right-handed, then fig. 14 shows that the forehand requires more green, or a wider line to reach its objective, whereas the backhand requires a much narrower line of approach.

Can the player be sure the line remains the same, when now the mat is moved up the rink as in fig. 15? A home player may know the rink and will make the adjustments for line and length. For a player unfamiliar with the green, he should stay with the line he knows is good for the longer length of jack. It is easier to make any adjustment from a known and proven line rather than experiment with the first bowl. If the line remains the same, then the only change required is that of weight or pace at which the bowl is delivered.

Bowls is a game of adjustments. Any

movement of the jack which shifts it from the centre line will require a bowler to find a new line and length. Some of these adjustments are minimal and these are the more difficult, and demand exceptional skill, which is why such fine judgement should not be left until a game situation exists. Practice allows a player the

correct feel for such tiny alterations. Some players are famous for playing particular shots; such consistency results from very clear mental messages, allied to positive pre-visualisation. Such an abundance of information increases the degree of confidence enormously, and consequently the level of consistency.

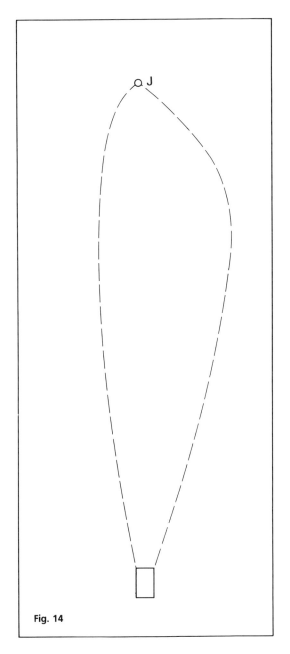

Fig. 14

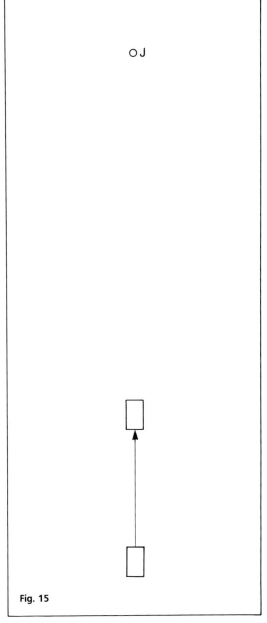

Fig. 15

WHAT COMES NEXT?

Assuming the playing surface has a fairly good and equal draw on both hands, a number of situations can be examined. It can also be assumed that the pace of the green has been measured over the required thirty yards and is running about twelve seconds. This represents the time taken by the bowl from the moment it leaves the hand to travel the thirty yards along the rink.

The slow green

Fig. 16 represents a slow green. The arc or line travelled by the bowl from mat to jack is quite narrow, therefore allowing it to cover the thirty yards in less time than on a fast green.

The fast green

Fig. 17 represents a fast green. The bowl requires a much wider arc or line than in fig. 16, and has further to travel. It needs longer time to cover the thirty yards.

Such information is important to the selection of shot. On a fast green a bowler would be able to draw past a short bowl, but would not find this so easily accomplished on a slower green.

Some available options

In fig. 18 player B can be faced with the following options:

■ drawing to rest against the opponent's bowl

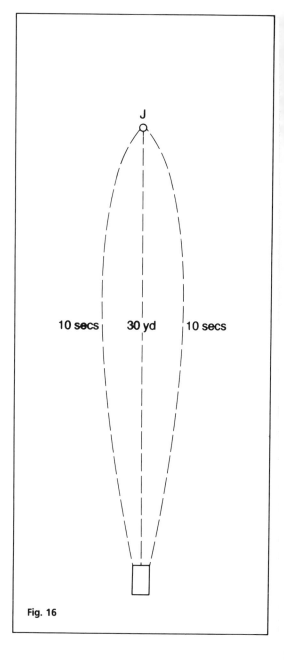

Fig. 16

- drawing to rest between the jack and the opponent's bowl
- drawing to the jack itself with a possibility of a 'toucher'.

All of these can be played on the forehand. Player B can still draw to the jack on the backhand but must attempt to bowl with exact length, rather than being heavy enough to push the jack towards his opponent's bowl. Being a fraction heavy on the forehand and making full contact with the jack could result in it being moved away from his opponent's bowl.

It is in player B's interest to deliver with

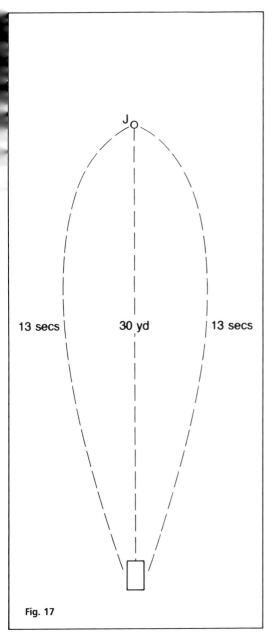

13 secs   30 yd   13 secs

Fig. 17

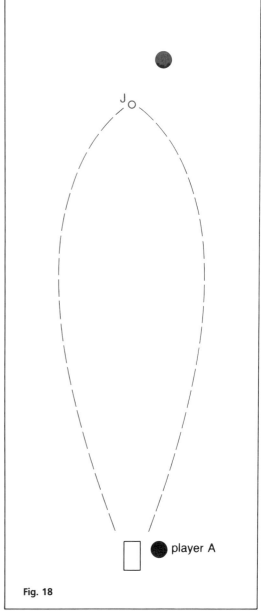

player A

Fig. 18

sufficient pace to reach the jack, since a bowl that ends up short could restrict his options for future shots.

In fig. 19 player A (black bowls) has begun to build a head very much in his favour. Player B could face a heavy count of shots against him,

unless he gives careful thought to the shot he is about to play. He has at least three options:

- to draw to the black bowl Y, just beyond jack high on the forehand
- to draw to the jack between bowls X and Y on the forehand
- to draw to the jack on the backhand where there are no bowls in the way.

Player B did not perform well with his first bowl, and now has to make an adjustment to weight or length. Weight or pace must be corrected very carefully to avoid an overcorrection so that the second bowl does not end up well beyond the jack. This is not as bad as his first bowl, but could allow the opponent to play his third bowl into a scoring position. In the game of singles, no player can allow a head to build against him. Usually the best response to such a situation is to play a shot which, although it may not be shot bowl, will at least give player B a bowl in the head.

Some bowlers may respond to this situation by using controlled weight in an attempt to break up the favourable position achieved by their opponent. It is important to gauge the pace of such a bowl carefully. Bowling beyond the head into the ditch without contact with the jack means the bowl is declared a 'dead bowl' and is wasted.

Playing the game of singles can place any bowler in a very lonely situation. There is no one else to assist. There is no one else to blame. There is no one else to take decisions. There is no one to guide, to encourage or to motivate. Playing the game of singles is a real test of character, of temperament and of dedication.

For any ambitious bowler who wishes to succeed as a singles player, every game is very important, and preparation and practice form integral ingredients to winning.

Fig. 19

TEAM PLAY

As well as the game of singles, there are several variations of team play in bowls.

First is the game of pairs, where the Lead and Skip each have four bowls to play over twenty-one ends. The game of triples comprises three players on each side, the Lead, Second and Skip, each playing three bowls over eighteen ends.

The game of rinks, sometimes referred to as four against four, has each player playing two bowls over twenty-one ends.

There are certain variations such as two-wood singles, or even two-wood pairs, but in the main these apply to specific tournaments.

Apart from County or National tournaments, there is the County League (usually rinks play) and even County Triples League. It is from participating in such league bowling that ambitious bowlers may go on to succeed at County or National level.

'You are just *that* much short!'

'Will it fall in?'

'This must be close'

'First part is good'

Playing Lead

When many bowlers first begin to play, they find themselves selected to play at Lead. The Lead has the responsibility for the correct placing of the mat, and more importantly, the casting of the jack. His job is to be as constant in drawing to the jack as his skill will allow. A good Lead is worth a great deal in pairs, triples or fours, because he provides the foundation for the building of the head.

Other playing positions

A player should remain at Lead to learn and reinforce the basic skills of the game before playing in a position such as a Third, or even a Skip. The position is one of great importance, demanding good bowling skills and providing an excellent school for development.

In the game of pairs, a Lead will complete four deliveries, and will then take his place at the head to work with his partner, the Skip. He will advise the Skip of any changes that may have occurred as well as direct him in the shot that may be required.

'I'll try this length of jack'

The marker will centre the jack

'Is that all right?'

'You can play it either hand'

A Lead has to understand the strengths and weaknesses in the head depending on the positioning of the bowls, and must work out all possible options.

The Skip should have every confidence in the ability of his Lead to inform him clearly and exactly of the prevailing position, so that he is better able to decide on his next shot.

There are occasions when the Lead can call the Skip up to the head so that the latter can have a better view of the positioning of the bowls. Such visits can result in discussion between the players as to the selection of the next shot. Such exchange of ideas, opinions, calculations and possible conclusions can form part of an excellent learning process.

Some players consider that an important attribute of a good Skip is a bowler who can fire effectively with one bowl, then execute a perfect draw with the next. What the player is demonstrating is that he is drawing on his store of past experience, and is better equipped to play certain shots than if he had remained

playing purely as a Lead. Even though a Lead may not be called upon to bowl a wide variety of shots, there is nothing to prevent that Lead from improving and extending his ability by carefully prepared practices.

Such practice is represented in fig. 20.

Shot 1. To draw the shot on the forehand.

Shot 2. To wrest bowl Y away from its scoring position.

Shot 3. To play on the backhand with sufficient weight so that bowl X is pushed into the ditch.

Shot 4. To draw to the edge of the ditch.

The practice offers a variety of line and length for each shot.

By setting up a mirror image of this exercise a player could then practise on the backhand. Any bowler can practise on his own, or seek the advice and assistance of a coach.

Regardless of the position a bowler may

'That's the weight you want'

It hasn't made it any easier!

occupy in Pairs, Triples or Fours, it is important that each game is used to broaden the learning process. Much can be learned, even from a game that was lost. Some bowlers like a detailed analysis of the whole game – win or lose – and keep a record of each head in detail so that post-match analysis is of greater value.

The majority of bowlers probably know where they went wrong and can only hope that they don't make the same mistakes again.

Others go to a game with a well formed plan in mind. If their plan works then all is well, but if the game is one of constant adjustment, then all players need to be able to adjust to any change in the original plan. To attempt to preserve a plan could amount to a degree of inflexibility that would play into the hands of any opponent. Any bowler could be in the position of having to reappraise the game after each bowl played by his opponent. Each bowl delivered can bring about change. The game is fluid, demanding decision making, whether for success or survival. A bowler could be faced with an opponent holding sufficient shots to win the game. Perhaps the positioning of the opponent's bowls prevents a draw shot being played; therefore, a decision is made to kill the end. This means delivering a bowl with sufficient pace to drive the jack out of the confines of the rink. If this is achieved, then the end must be replayed. This sort of shot can be looked upon as a last resort, but never one to be played in a reckless fashion. Physical co-ordination and mental application must be spot on for such a shot to succeed.

Gaining a psychological advantage over your opponent is important in singles, pairs, triples or fours. If a team of bowlers look despondent, this may well boost the confidence of the opposition. The following examples show situations when commonsense should prevail.

Positions at the head

In fig. 21 player A has one bowl left, and is holding shot with bowl A. The slightest movement of the jack could result in him losing shots, because he has no bowl over jack high and player B has bowls in a receiving position. Player A should decide not to bowl, because if the shot goes wrong, a scoring and psychological advantage will be handed to his opponent.

In fig. 22 player B is holding shot with bowl X but has three more bowls in a good receiving position should the jack be moved. Player A

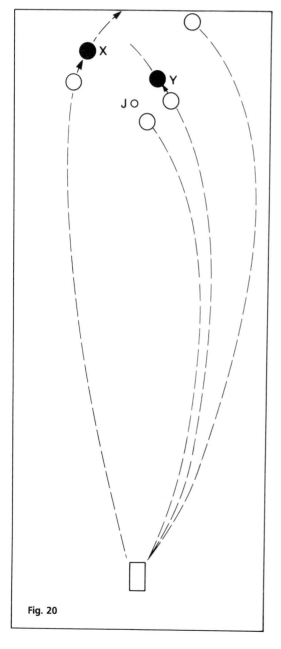

Fig. 20

holds second shot with bowl D. A minimal error of judgement by him in attempting to gain the shot could result in player B scoring more than the one shot he already holds. Commonsense should dictate that player A does not bowl his last bowl and allows one shot to be counted for player B.

Of course, if player B was actually holding game with bowl X, then player A would adopt quite a different approach. He could attempt to kill the end, or indeed to play with controlled weight on to his own bowl D, hoping to push it on to the jack for the jack to make contact with bowl X and therefore be squeezed out of the

player B
player A

Fig. 21

Fig. 22

head. Under such circumstances it does not matter whether player A loses by just one or four shots; he cannot afford to leave the situation as it is.

After the game

Games can be won or lost for many different reasons. Quite simply, a bowler could be faced with an opponent whose natural ability and range of skills is better than his own. What is galling for any bowler is not to perform well; to play well below the normal level of performance. A number of factors could be responsible, and will need to be recognised. They must be included in all post-match considerations because only then can they be amended or eliminated before the next important game.

If the main reason for defeat is a lack of confidence and consistency in a certain area of the game, or certain shots, a player could seek to work with a qualified coach. A coach will be the best person to assist in improving your game (see 'Goal setting', page 40).

Good or bad luck never seems to be present in equal amounts. There is nothing that you can do about either, therefore there is no point in gloating over the first or bemoaning the latter.

One syndrome that needs to be guarded against is that of euphoria. Many games have been lost by players who have experienced this feeling when they find themselves well in the lead. The danger is that concentration will be lost, and once gone, is difficult to recover. Any post-mortem following a game needs to be constructive. From any such discussion positive information and details must be gathered that can be included in the planning for improvement in future performance. Remember that as much can be learned from victory as from defeat. All positive attributes should be reinforced during a post-match discussion to increase the confidence of any bowler.

During an important game of singles a famous bowler dropped the maximum count of four shots. The next end saw this bowler gain a maximum count of four. The rationale that was offered was that when losing four shots, he could see that the four bowls he had played were not all that bad, and this very positive attitude was employed during the playing of the next end. Equally, it could be suggested that his opponent has allowed a maximum success to dent his concentration.

There could have been a combination of the above, but all bowlers must accept that the most important bowl in any game is the one that you are preparing to play. The bowler mentioned above did not allow any kind of negative thinking to distract him from the task in hand; and his reward was a full count against his opponent.

COMMON FAULTS

Delivery action

One of the most important areas of assistance to bowlers offered by the English Bowls Coaching Scheme is that of the delivery clinic. Such clinics have proved their worth in helping many hundreds of bowlers eradicate certain faults that they have developed in their delivery action. Some of these clinics are aided by the use of video, which provides an instant replay on a split screen television facility. This immensely important visual aid can show a bowler exactly where his delivery is letting him down.

Many people who attend such coaching sessions do so because of the problem of stiffening limbs and joints. Working together, coach and bowler can produce a quite different delivery action which allows the bowler to play with less discomfort or margin of error.

Grip

It is best to hold the bowl comfortably in the hand, rather than attempt to exert pressure with thumb or fingers. As a general guideline, you should use as large a bowl as is comfortable for your hand. This demands careful and considered selection.

There are two forms of grip, **claw** and **cradle**, and there are numerous variations between the two types.

Strength of wrist, hand and fingers, as well as the length of fingers and thumb, all have their

The real importance of the grip is that it works for you. The next seven photographs show some variations which have proved consistently successful for the individuals concerned

part to play in determining the grip of any individual. It could be to some advantage to have as much of the hand as possible in contact with the bowl. This facilitates the smooth rolling of the bowl off the fingers.

The top left photograph opposite shows the thumb well on top of the bowl. For those who can deliver the bowl smoothly by using this grip, then all is well. However, you should avoid applying a great deal of pressure with the

thumb. This sometimes results in a whiteness of the skin at the base and top of the thumb as well as the wrist. The bowl may also be put into, rather than rolled along, the playing surface.

Since no two delivery actions are exactly the same, this also applies to the form of the grip. Many bowlers hold the bowl in their own individual fashion. The important point to remember is that it suits them and may not suit another bowler.

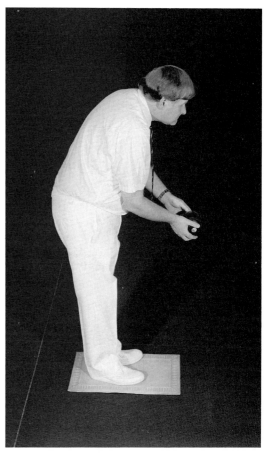

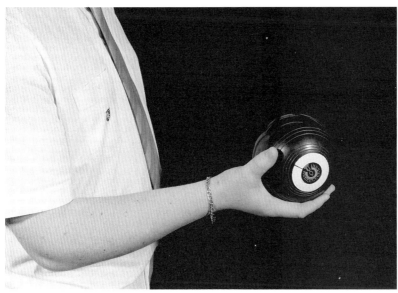

Fingers are usually placed parallel to the running surface. Placing the little finger too high on the side of the bowl can cause a slight wobble on release. Such placing of the little finger is often related to the positioning of the thumb. It is sometimes used as a counter-balance when the thumb is high or on top of the bowl. If a slight wobble does occur, it is time to think again about the way you hold the bowl.

When a coach advises a player to reposition his thumb, so he is now holding the bowl as opposed to gripping it, he may feel a lack of control. Yet it is evident that the method employed of holding or gripping a bowl can have a direct effect upon the bowl at the moment of release.

Another important consideration is that the bowl should be held upright in the hand and not inclined either to the left or to the right. From the centre line of the bowl in the hand, an imaginary line should extend back along the arm to the elbow joint. A bowl not held upright is not delivered on the full running surface and

may not behave in the way a player expects it to.

Grip is an integral part of the delivery action. If it is not correct, then the delivery of the bowl will be less than satisfactory. It is important that all bowlers find the grip best suited to them and which allows a smooth and error-free delivery.

Stance

Within the extremes of upright and fixed, there are a number of variations of stance adopted by players. As with grip, there is essentially no right or wrong form. The chosen stance will be best suited to a particular player depending upon weight and build. Those players who experience some stiffness in hip or knee joints may have to adopt a stance of compromise to enable them to release the bowl smoothly.

Every stance needs to provide the bowler with a relaxed and well balanced platform for the delivery of the bowl. Those who place their

A fixed stance

A deep crouch

feet very close together could be limiting the area of balance. It might be better to have the feet slightly apart, so that body weight is borne evenly. However, feet placed too wide apart could bring problems when the forward step is taken for the delivery of the bowl. Therefore, it is important to think carefully about the placing and spacing of the feet to provide the best possible balanced position.

Whichever stance is adopted, it is important that the player turns the whole body to face the correct line for playing the shot. Most bowlers judge that line from an object on the opposite bank or a particular spot on the green. From whichever point of reference, the next most important thing is for the player to place his right foot, for a right-handed player, pointed exactly at that spot. The left foot can then be

Slightly less than upright stance

Variation on the fixed
stance

A three-legged stool

placed in its appropriate position to enable the player to align the whole body to the required line, as well as having an evenly balanced position on the mat.

Stance is crucial to the completion of a successful delivery. Because the bowl travels in a curved line, the body needs to be angled away from the spot where the bowler wishes his bowl to come to rest. The correct angle will be found more easily by taking a quite deliberate stance on the mat.

Some bowlers have adopted a stance which seems difficult for others to follow. Frequently, such a stance is part of that particular player's ritual of delivery and may be his way of feeling comfortable and confident before the bowl leaves the hand. Many of the top bowlers allow a certain amount of time after adopting their stance before actually releasing the bowl. This brief period of a few seconds may enable them to completely focus their concentration on the shot to be played.

From taking up your stance, to the release of the bowl, it is as well to limit all physical movements to the barest minimum. There is no point in destroying a deliberate and well balanced stance by introducing any extra physical actions that could upset it. Always keep it simple.

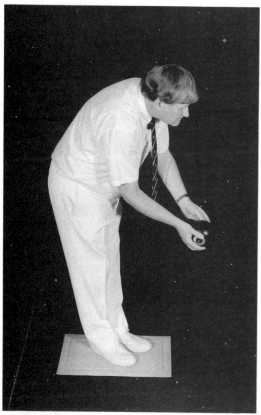

A well-balanced stance

Backswing

All that is required for the backswing is to move the bowling arm backwards in an arc or pendulum movement. Before starting your backswing, it is important to think where the bowl is being held in relation to the body. Some bowlers hold the bowl away from the body so that during the backswing they allow it to travel further away or try to bring it closer to the hip. Neither of these actions is particularly good, since they can cause a loss of line or, indeed, a less than satisfactory release of the bowl.

Others hold the bowl in front of the body and during the backswing have to negotiate the hip. This action can again result in the bowl moving away from the body. With an overcorrection at the end of the backswing the bowl can be tucked away behind the body of the player. Whichever is the case, another correction will have to be made before the bowl is released to bring the bowling arm forward as close to the body as possible. It is better for the elbow of the bowling arm to rest close to the hip, and the bowl held so that it is pointing along the correct line.

Experience at coaching clinics has shown that bowlers generally have widely different views about the backswing. Most will agree that it is important to keep the bowling arm comfortably close to the body, but the differences appear when the length of backswing comes under discussion. Many are adamant that the length the bowl travels is in direct proportion to the length of the backswing, but are not quite so certain as to how long the increased length of backswing should be. There are several players from the southern hemisphere who demonstrate quite extended backswings, but can still play a delicate draw to a minumum length jack. There is also the added problem when attempting to bowl with increased pace, that the backswing is performed at an increased speed. Most players have a quite natural length of backswing which is an essential part of their delivery action. Perhaps it is as well to keep to this regular and natural length, then, if delivering a bowl with increased pace, simply speed up the forward swing. Here, care must be taken to deliver the bowl smoothly and not to accompany it with a forward lunge of the body since this can lead to loss of balance at the precise second when everything should be just right.

A brief backswing

A slightly longer backswing than Allcock's

Richard Bray's backswing

Some players twist their wrist during the backswing so that the back of the bowling hand is close to the body. This could be a personal quirk, or an attempt to prevent the bowl from moving away from the body, but it must not be forgotten that the wrist has to be untwisted during the forward swing so that the bowl can be grounded smoothly on its running surface. A backswing is simply a pendulum movement and for many bowlers any twisting action of the wrist will only be a complication to what is essentially a straightforward movement.

The well known bowler David Bryant, C.B.E., twists his wrist during his backswing. Although this action obviously works for him, it may not work for others.

The forward swing

The speed of the bowling arm during the forward swing must be gauged precisely to the distance that the bowl needs to travel. One common fault that can occur is for the bowler to accelerate the speed of the bowling arm over the last foot or so of the arc. This can result in a bowl being lobbed out of the hand rather than

Good completion of the forward swing

Nothing apart from the arm moves

being grounded smoothly. Such sudden acceleration can mean the bowling arm being on its way upwards before the bowl is released from the hand.

Apart from those bowlers who adopt a fixed stance and only need move the bowling arm, the majority have to include other body movements with the forward swing. The first is to lower the body so that, at the moment of release, the bowling hand is as close as possible to the playing surface. If this is not achieved then the bowl will be bumped on release. Lowering the body can be greatly assisted if bowlers bend their knees slightly, even before they begin the backswing.

During the forward swing the bowling arm needs to be as close to the body as possible, with the arm exactly on the correct line.

Many bowlers combine a forward step with their swing, so it is important that all movements are carefully co-ordinated. This co-ordination is better if the original stance is balanced.

One movement that several players synchronise with the forward swing is placing their non-bowling hand on the knee of the leg with which they make the forward step. Some grasp the knee, while others allow the hand to rest lightly just above it. It is advisable not to treat this as support for the upper body, but more to reduce any nuisance the non-bowling arm could offer.

The forward swing, with its accompanying body movements, is very important to a good delivery. Any slight imbalance during the swing could mean a poor result. Great care and good control must be the keynote. It must be a deliberate and disciplined movement, with the bowl being released fractionally ahead of the forward foot.

When it is necessary to bowl with increased weight, the forward swing should increase in speed. Because of this speeding up, the exact moment of release must be judged carefully. There must be just as smooth a release as for a delicate drawing shot.

During the backward and forward swing, it is important that the shoulder, elbow, wrist and hand of the bowling arm do not vary from the chosen line.

The forward step

Some bowlers will take a forward step simultaneously with the backswing, whilst others will take it with the forward swing. This is a matter of choice, but it must be remembered that the forward step provides the platform for a good delivery. Usually, the length of the step need not be greater than a normal walking pace. Overstepping can result in a great deal of body weight being imparted into the delivery action. This could result in a loss of balance at the moment of release and the bowl being bumped along the playing surface.

It is sometimes argued that a longer forward stride is necessary when playing on a heavy or slow green. Longer need not mean stretching out the leg to the maximum distance. If the argument is correct, then it is important to bear in mind that the positioning of the leading foot is essential to overall balance. Any over-striding is not generally conducive to a good delivery.

To maintain good balance the foot should not be placed directly in front of the back foot, since this will provide too narrow a base. Nor should the leading foot be angled across the body as this could result in a loss of line as well as introducing a hooking action into the delivery.

The leading foot should remain parallel to a line extended from the back foot and parallel to the direction of the required line.

A variation is that some players place the forward foot some eight or ten inches ahead of the back foot even before they begin the backswing. The completion of this stride forward will occur during the forward swing. The distance the forward foot will need to be moved is now minimal. Some players think this stance gives them better balance and enables them to bowl consistently well. Others think that if a flexing of the knees is also incorporated, then this can lead to an even smoother delivery.

Coaching experience has proved that if a bowler bends the knees prior to backswing, and by so doing lowers the body, then it is more difficult to take a long forward stride. Of course, during the backswing and forward swing the body needs to be kept in the lowered position

Tony Allcock is beautifully balanced for a smooth delivery of the bowl

A firm foundation

A shorter forward stride

'Wrong' foot forward, but a good delivery

without raising the upper half of the body. If this happens then it is easier to take a longer forward stride.

The release

The timing of the release is very important for the successful delivery of any bowl. A fraction too early or too late will mean the bowl being bumped as it leaves the hand. It is essential to lower the body as close as possible to the playing surface and this action can be practised at home by going through a delivery action without a bowl, making sure that the fingers brush the carpet.

The bowl should be released at approximately six to nine inches ahead of the leading foot, with the body facing the required line and the head kept still. The bowl should be rolled off the platform provided by the hand.

One common fault with many bowlers is that at the precise moment of release there is an unnecessary flick of the wrist which does not allow the bowl to be delivered with the smoothness essential for a good result.

A well-delivered bowl

A very smooth delivery

A good release from a fixed stance

Follow through

The follow through should be a natural completion of the pendulum movement of the forward swing. To remind yourself of this action, place a coin in the middle of your hand where fingers meet the palm, then by a pendulum movement of the arm, lob the coin gently out of the hand. Your hand will be palm uppermost and the arm pointing along your chosen line.

A common fault is a twisting of the wrist either inward or outward, depending upon the hand that is being played. This is not conducive to a good follow through and can result in a bowl being wobbled on release.

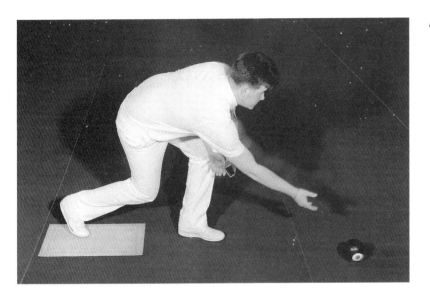

A smooth follow through

An individual style of follow through

The Allcock follow through

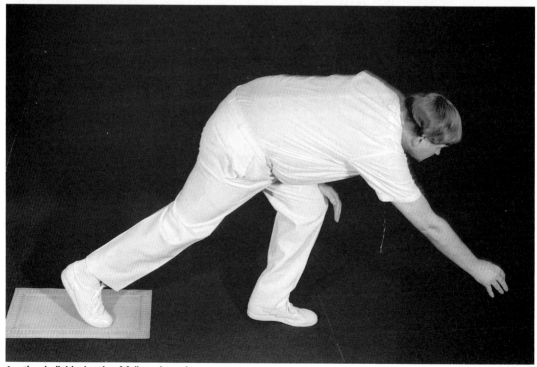

Another individual style of follow through

The high completion point

On follow through many bowlers bring their bowling arm across the body. If the bowl has already left the hand, then probably no harm is done. However, to begin this sweeping action a split second too soon can cause the delivery of the bowl to be less than effective.

Any form of follow through will not be attained if body balance is incorrect. Players not properly balanced could find that just after release of the bowl, their bowling arm may need to be used as a prop to stop themselves falling.

Since there are many variations in delivery action, the same applies to any follow through. There are very successful bowlers who employ little or no follow through, therefore each player must find the action best suited to his delivery style.

The bowler's head and eyes are along the line of the bowl

The bowler is comfortable and relaxed

Position of the head

All bowlers are aware of the importance of keeping the head still during the delivery action. Many faults in the delivery of a bowl can be traced directly to unnecessary movements of the head.

Try to avoid bobbing your head upwards at the moment of release. This swift lifting action will transfer itself to the neck, shoulders and arms, and is a contributory cause to the bowl being bumped on delivery.

If you have developed this head lifting fault, a coach may advise that you discipline yourself to watch the bowl travel along the green for something between eight or ten yards. By keeping your eyes on the bowl, it is easy to overcome this particular fault. You will also feel much better balanced by keeping your head quite still for this length of time after the bowl is on its way.

Some players drop their head when the forward swing is almost complete and because of this have problems in bowling a consistent line. Practise bowling to one particular spot; keeping your eyes directly on this spot can alleviate this problem. The exercise can last until you begin to feel the correct angle of head and neck.

Faults usually develop over a long period of time and will not always be eradicated or corrected quickly. The coach and especially the bowler will have to work hard at finding the correct solution.

Another problem that can arise is the head being held too high and rigid. Although you should keep your head still, if it is held in an uncomfortable position, this will result in tension in the neck and shoulders which can transfer itself to the bowling arm. Since players generally have an optimum distance which they can look along the rink in comfort, it is not advisable to look beyond this point.

To help a player in this position, a coach should first ascertain the point on the opposite bank that the player has chosen. He will then ask the bowler to adopt the appropriate stance on the mat and begin to walk towards the player from the other end of the rink. The coach will ask the player to tell him when he has

The head is held perfectly still on delivery of the bowl

reached a point where the bowler can look at him with ease. A marker is then put on that spot and the bowler bowls over it. The coach will mark at different distances to find the distance best suited to the bowler who will then bowl repeatedly over the indicated mark until he gets the feel of the different positions of head, neck and shoulders.

The non-bowling arm

Since the whole body is directly involved in all delivery actions, you cannot ignore the non-bowling arm.

Many bowlers allow this arm to be free and keep it in the same position for each delivery. If this does not happen, the delivery action will not be as well synchronised as it should be.

Support for the non-bowling arm

Some keep this arm firmly at their side, whilst others fling it backwards simultaneously with the forward swing. The latter action must be strictly controlled or it may result in a loss of balance.

The majority of bowlers rest their non-bowling arm on the forward leg, but by no means all in the same fashion. Some allow the hand and arm to rest lightly on the thigh or knee; others grasp the knee firmly and use the non-bowling arm as a support for the upper part of the body. However, in both cases, the non-bowling arm is not allowed to wave about and create problems such as loss of balance.

There is no hard and fast rule as to the positioning of the non-bowling arm, but the importance of exercising control over both the arm and hand cannot be emphasised enough.

The rear leg and foot

Under normal circumstances, the rear leg is the right leg for right-handed players, and the opposite for a left-handed delivery.

Here the non-bowling arm rests lightly on the left knee

The rear leg is slightly behind the forward leg

However, there are a number of bowlers who bowl from the 'wrong' foot. That is to say, a right-handed player may step forward with the right foot. There is no ruling to say that this is not acceptable. That particular bowler is delivering the bowl in a fashion best suited to him. However, the position of the rear foot needs to conform to Law 27 of the English Bowling Association rules which states that any bowler, when delivering the jack or bowl, *'shall have one foot remaining entirely within the confines of the mat. The foot may be either in contact with, or over the mat. Failure to observe this law constitutes foot faulting'*.

Many players raise their back leg at the moment of release. As long as the positioning of the foot conforms to the above rule, all is well. The raising of the back foot imparts a

The extravagance of youth!

greater amount of body weight into the delivery action and therefore needs to be well controlled. Also the weight of the body is transferred to the leading foot and care must be taken to prevent loss of balance.

Any bowler who thinks his game is suffering from any of these common faults should seek assistance and advice from a coach qualified under the English Bowls Coaching Scheme. Such a coach will be able to offer remedial advice, but it is the player who is faced with the hard work required to eliminate the fault. In some cases coaching sessions can be quite brief and improvement immediate. Others will require a longer period of time and application, but the results could be well worth the efforts of coach and player.

The player bowls from a firm foundation

POSITIONS IN THE GAME

The Lead

The Lead in the game of pairs, triples or fours has a very important contribution to make. The Lead will need to be a player who can demonstrate consistently accurate drawing skill.

In any first end, the mat is placed according to rule. The Lead then takes up his stance on the mat, looks carefully at where his Skip is standing, and prepares to deliver the jack to that point. A Lead who can deliver the jack with consistent accuracy makes an important contribution, even before a bowl has been played.

During subsequent ends, the Skip may request the Lead to move the mat further up or back along the rink, as allowed by rule. This ploy is used to perhaps disturb the rhythm of opponents, or to test them out. However, no matter where the mat is placed, the Lead has to deliver the jack to the length requested by his Skip. There is little point in moving the mat well up the green if the jack is then badly delivered and ends up in the ditch.

Having correctly delivered the jack, the Lead must prepare to bowl the first bowl of the end. He will wish it to be close to the jack, possibly in front or slightly behind, or even at jack high.

John Ottaway, Lead for England

A good bowl will put pressure on the opponents. The Lead will set the pattern for the development of the head, and with a good first bowl he will establish a confident approach which will soon spread to the other players to boost their confidence.

With his second bowl a Lead may receive instructions from his Skip, depending upon what has happened as a result of the opponent's first bowl. Where the opponent's bowl has made no difference at all, the Lead should try to produce a repeat performance of his first bowl. He should be equally determined to deliver a good second bowl. If he succeeds, then he has provided his rink with a sound foundation for the building of the head.

Providing that his rink wins the end, the Lead will prepare himself yet again to place the mat and deliver the jack. Some players use a quite different style of grip for delivering the jack, some even holding their first bowl with their non-bowling hand. This action allows the Lead to remain standing on the mat, watch the jack run its course, and then simply transfer the bowl to the other hand in readiness to play. In short, he has not needed to leave the mat at all.

In many cases there may be a gap of eight to ten minutes between the delivery of the last of the Lead's bowls and the beginning of the next end. This is the time when it is easy to lose concentration. It is not really feasible for concentration to be sustained throughout, but the Lead should endeavour to be watchful and interested in all play. He should encourage his fellow players; demonstrate and share his confidence in them; make his own contribution to the ethos of the rink and its compatibility. Some players who prefer to play at Lead could still have a sound knowledge of tactics, strategy and shot selection, and could be encouraged by the Skip to make their own contribution whenever consultation takes place. The important point is that the Lead must maintain a complete involvement at all stages of the game.

The vast majority of the shots played by a Lead will be variations on the draw shot. Even if his opponent has bowled a front toucher, then the shot required to free the jack is essentially drawing to a point behind it so that the bowl will make contact with his opponent's bowl with just sufficient pace to free the jack.

The Second (number two)

It is reasonable to assume that the Second may be asked to play a far greater variety of shots than would usually be expected from a Lead. If the Lead does not perform well, it may be up to the Second to retrieve the situation for his rink.

The Skip may want nothing more than for the Second to bowl the shot bowl, or at least a good second bowl. The Second may not have as clear a sight of the jack as the Lead had. The positioning of the four bowls already played could prove some hindrance to a straightforward drawing shot to the jack. Sometimes the situation at the head is such that the Skip may invite the Second to visit the head so that he can gain a clearer picture of the shot to be played. Any Skip needs to be able to rely upon his Number Two to retrieve a situation. In the majority of cases this would be asking the player to demonstrate good drawing skills. The Second must be able to produce scoring bowls if the Lead has failed to accomplish this, and therefore he must be expert at the draw shot.

When the Lead has done his part well, the Second will be asked to consolidate the position and will attempt to bowl exactly as requested by his Skip. Such bowls are described as positional bowls. If the Skip needs a bowl a good yard beyond the jack, then the Second must draw to that point. With his second bowl, he could be asked to hit an opponent's bowl with just sufficient pace to move it from its position. This again is a variation of the draw shot, and if well executed can increase the pressure on the opposition.

According to the position at the head, the Second may be requested to play those shots which are nothing more than variations on the draw shot. He may be asked to play a promotion shot; a trail shot to move the jack a required distance; or a shot to a front toucher so that the jack is sprung into full view. With all of these, he must be confident of bowling along the correct line and with exact pace or weight. Even if he does not achieve the perfect result, he must ensure that his bowl comes to rest where it could still be of some value to his rink. Therefore the Number Two must perfect his shots, particularly where he has to make a

'Will it spring the jack?'

minimal adjustment to increase the pace very slightly. Such shots are very demanding and call for a high level of skill.

All those who play at Number Two carry the score card and at the completion of each end, when the number of shots for or against has been determined, they must enter this information on the card. It is valuable to compare notes with the opposing Number Two after each end to ensure the correct scores are recorded. The Second may also be requested to update the score board at the end of the rink which is visible to players and spectators alike.

As with the other players in the rink, the Number Two must be supportive of the others, and may be invited to join in the discussion that can take place with regard to the selection of the next shot to be played. This is a recognition of his knowledge of the game, so it is clear that a good Second can offer a whole range of positive attributes to the rink, though most important of all will be his skill as a bowler.

The Third (number three)

A good Third will need to establish a good playing and personal understanding with the Lead and Second as well as with the Skip. He is there for the benefit of the whole rink. He must relate to all of the players in the rink if he is to fulfil his function as a good Third.

It may seem obvious to state that the Third should be supportive of his Skip but, equally, he may have a point of view with regard to selection of shot that is different from the Skip. The Third must accept that if his suggestion as to the selection of shot is not accepted, no slight is intended. It is simply a question of there being two different opinions, and the Skip reserves the right to make the final decision.

Some bowlers see the bonding between Third and Skip as one of the most important attributes of a good rink. The head must be built, shots must be selected and decided upon, and most importantly they have to be played. It

is obviously better if the Skip and his Third agree completely on the forthcoming shot, but even if the Third has some reservations, he must play to the best of his ability and comply with the Skip.

The Third needs to play a very wide variety of shots, ranging from the perfect drawing shot to a shot played with weight, perhaps to open up the head. This brings in another aspect of a Third's game – he must be totally unselfish in his approach and know and understand that whatever shot he has been asked to play is ultimately for the good of the rink as a whole.

When the Skip has left the head and is preparing to play a shot, this is *not* the time for the Third to talk or point to particular bowls. Some Skips take a moment or two to compose themselves before playing the shot, and this is sometimes mistaken for hesitation by some Thirds who feel it necessary to issue further information. If the Skip requires any information, then he will ask for it. If the Skip is at the mat end when his opponent has

'That's the bowl to reach'

completed his shot, and cannot see the head well, then he may request the Third to tell him of any change. This feedback to the Skip must be done succinctly and with clarity, and can be described as one of the most demanding areas of good Third play. All communication should be clear and precise.

A Third should be able to read the head well. He should be totally aware of the position and juxtaposition of bowls and be able to assess all areas of strengths and weaknesses in and around the head. He must appreciate positions where shots can be gained or lost, and inform the Skip accordingly. The Third must have the total confidence of the Skip. Any shot suggested by the Third should be confidently played by the Skip. There may be occasions when the position is a tight one, where the Third will invite the Skip to come and look at the head.

On completion of the end, if the Third's rink has scored, it is advisable to allow the opposing Third to remove the shot or shots. Both Thirds should be vigilant in making quite sure that

there are no more shots to count – one way or the other. Obviously, where there is any doubt, then a measure will be used. A good Third must be thoroughly conversant with the use of the measure. If, in the event, the opposing Thirds are unable to agree after having measured, then the Skips will be invited to decide. If there is still no agreement, then an Umpire will be called, and his decision will be accepted as final.

Some players view the Third as a counterpart to the Skip. A too exuberant attitude by a Third might be upsetting for some Skips and welcomed by others, so it is important that the Third gain the complete confidence and trust of the Skip. Then, each will play at his best.

It is sometimes felt that a Third might play the majority of his shots with added weight. This is not necessarily correct, for he may be asked to play a variety of shots in order to retrieve, to consolidate or to protect the head. Most will be variations on the draw shot, and the Third must attempt to become master of them all.

'We want that one out'

The umpire's decision is final

The good Third has many parts to play and will contribute much to the total well-being and ethos of the rink. His position is one of great responsibility so a good Third will be an enormous attribute in the rinks game.

The Skip

This is a position in the rink that many bowlers aspire to reach as soon as they can and, in some cases, too soon. Playing at Skip seems to carry some accolade of accomplishment, acceptability, recognition and respect. However, respect does not come with the title, but must be earned.

Those who play in this position take upon themselves several areas of responsibility even before a bowl is played. The Skip has much to contribute to his fellow players in order to promote and encourage that degree of compatibility that is so essential to the well-being of the rink. Even so, it must be remembered that all players should play well with, and for, each other. In short, play as a team and not simply as four individuals.

If bowlers were asked to list all the qualities they would expect any Skip to demonstrate, they may be surprised at the length of the list.

'An excellent bowl!'

'We are holding one!'

'It would be difficult to get in there!'

'Has he got enough weight?'

Briefly, the Skip needs to be all things to all people. He needs to be able to sum up the players in his rink, to learn quickly how he will guide, compose, motivate, encourage, reward, console, congratulate and consequently do all that he can to bring out the best performance possible from each player.

In bowling terms, he must learn their strengths and weaknesses, and exploit all positive elements to the full. He must be clear and concise in all instructions. Any indecision will transfer itself to the player waiting to play the shot. He must attempt to be a master of strategy and tactics. He must be well versed in reading the head, as well as exploiting the options on offer. He must know when to introduce caution, as well as the time to be courageous.

At the same time, he must seek to find out all that he can about his opponents. He must strive to gain any psychological advantage that is possible, without the slightest hint of

Plenty of room to draw

gamesmanship. He must try to read his opponents' game as much as his own, and be ready to forecast their reaction to any given situation. Information about their style of play and any response to a particular situation at the head is necessary for making decisions.

With regard to decision making, he may confer with the Third only, or he may involve the other players and arrive at a collective decision. He must judge the precise time to confer, to listen, and to make his own views known, and not offend any of his players who may have offered quite different views.

An important part of gaining the confidence and trust of his rink must rest with the playing ability of the Skip. He must demonstrate confidence and consistency in any shot in the game, and should be master of most. To achieve this, the player who aspires to Skip must prepare himself as thoroughly as possible. This means practice, followed by more practice, especially in his weak areas. A Skip who bowls

Every picture tells a story!

and achieves the best result possible can boost the morale of his players.

A Skip needs to remember that his own players are watching and reading him most carefully. If their assessment results in a good and positive profile, then they will be far more supportive of him because he has gained their trust and confidence – he has been judged as much as a person as a player.

The Skip should also bear in mind that his team members have their own characteristics as people. Their pattern of behaviour could be a positive asset to the rink, especially if the Skip is clever enough to channel this behaviour to the benefit of the others. The natural exuberance of one player could be cancelled out by another being introvert. The Skip must use quite different approaches with each to make them feel a sense of belonging to the rink as a whole. Comments to each player should be tailored exactly to their needs and yet appear to be quite spontaneous utterances.

Most Skips are not trained sports psychologists, but will have to behave as though they were to get the best from all of the players in the rink. Those who wish to play as a Skip must demonstrate leadership qualities that inspire others to play above themselves. This is not evident in all Skips, but they should at least demonstrate sound commonsense.

Leadership need not always be lonely, especially if the Skip does not set himself apart from his rink. The Skip should always show the keenest interest in his team-mates. Disinterest is the greatest discourtesy. Players want their Skip to be aware, alert and alive to their every need. If this is achieved they will be better able to support him throughout the game and will welcome the opportunity of playing in his rink again.

'He might find the gap'

THE GAME OF BOWLS

As with other games, bowls should provide a great source of enjoyment as well as the opportunity for each player to perform to the best of his potential. It appears to be a game that can be played in quiet and calm, needs to be methodical and measured, disciplined and deliberate, requires great skill, and yet seems not to place any great physical demand on any player.

However, the game of bowls can arouse a wide range of emotions. There will be moments of deep disappointment or great joy, despair or euphoria. It can demand courage, control, concentration and caution, as well as delicacy and decisiveness.

Players should demonstrate determination while still recognising an opponent's skill in the manner of true sportsmanship.

Mental application must be strict in erasing any negative thoughts and ignoring any form of distraction.

Bowls requires total involvement from its players. It seeks compatibility between players as well as trust and confidence in decision making.

It provides friendship and comradeship. It offers contacts across a wide age range and helps to promote a greater acceptance and understanding of others, regardless of age.

(a) A long backswing

It can provide a form of gentle relaxation or intense rivalry and the challenge of pitting skill against skill. Such skills may cover a wide range of ability, but there is plenty of scope for even the most ambitious bowler to demonstrate his mastery of the game.

(b) The forward swing with added bodyweight

(c) A well-played shot

INDEX